## More Praise for *Leadership from the Inside Out*

"Research on leadership is clear: leaders must move from task-specific expertise to personal, interpersonal, and strategic excellence to succeed. Cashman's *Leadership from the Inside Out* gives you both deep and pragmatic practices to help make this crucial leadership transition."
—Kenneth R. Brousseau, PhD, CEO, Decision Dynamics LLC

"Kevin Cashman knows people can change, but to really improve the outside, every person needs to understand what's on the inside. This book walks you through a step-by-step process of self-discovery. Anyone who is serious about personal improvement should contemplate the questions posed by this book."
—Joseph Folkman, coauthor of *The Extraordinary Leader*

"Kevin Cashman's message of staying resilient is critically relevant in today's high-change, high-stress marketplace. *Leadership from the Inside Out* provides a set of tools for managing energy and personal engagement, crucial to stay ahead of the game of leading and living."
—Jim Loehr, CEO, Human Performance Institute, and coauthor of *The Power of Full Engagement*

"Sooner or later, every leader who would like to lead more effectively finds himself blocked. Kevin Cashman's book illuminates how we can find the means within ourselves to identify and remove these barriers in order to fulfill our leadership destiny."
—J.P. Donlon, Editor-in-Chief, *Chief Executive*

"As leaders, we all need to grow from technical-functional expertise to personal-interpersonal excellence. *Leadership from the Inside Out* shows us impactful ways to take this journey with integrity and respect for all those we serve."
—Juergen Brokatzky-Geiger, PhD, Head of Human Resources, Novartis International AG

"Bolstered by strong science and the refined art of leadership development, few books so clearly bring the many aspects of our lives into alignment. Whether you're taking your own talent or that of others to the next level, *Leadership from the Inside Out* provides an abundance of tools for authentic, long-term success."
—Ana Dutra, CEO, Leadership Development Solutions, Korn/Ferry International

"No matter your professional arena, self-understanding and team trust are key to enduring success. *Leadership from the Inside Out* has brought out the best in our team, showing how our far-reaching talents, values, and experiences all directly fuel performance."
—Mark Cohon, Commissioner, Canadian Football League

"*Leadership from the Inside Out* has produced something any manager should admire: long-term value. As a former national bestseller and perennial member on our monthly bestseller list, Cashman's classic has provoked positive change in leaders of all types and backgrounds for years. This revised and expanded work takes the timeless principles first introduced ten years ago and brings them to life for the next generation of leaders through new examples, new research, and new meaning."
—Jack Covert, President and Founder, 800-CEO-READ

"*Leadership from the Inside Out* serves as an important wake-up call for those who are ready to unleash the power of authentic leadership."
—Ken Melrose, University of St. Thomas Holloran Endowed Chair in the Practice of Management; former Chairman and CEO, The Toro Company; and author of *Making the Grass Greener on Your Side: A CEO's Journey to Leading by Serving*

"True adventure always involves the exploration of one's innermost spirit. *Leadership from the Inside Out* is a compass that helps you navigate this hidden domain as a means to bring out full leadership capacity with honesty and renewed energy."
—Ann Bancroft, polar explorer (first woman to reach the North and South Poles) and Founder, Ann Bancroft Foundation

"If you want personal transformation, then buy *Leadership from the Inside Out*. It will guide you through the unexplored territories we often miss in our frenetic-paced business world."
—Trudy Rautio, Executive Vice President and CFO, Carlson Hospitality Worldwide

"*Leadership from the Inside Out* is a testament to the too often forgotten reality that leadership success comes from living your deepest purpose and values as you earn followers, starting with the person in the mirror."
—Vance Caesar, PhD, leadership coach and mentor, The Vance Caesar Group, and Professor, Pepperdine University

"In the dozen years I have known Kevin Cashman, he has consistently made his work a masterpiece in the art of leading on purpose. His new edition is an intriguing guide to this art, and it inspires us to take it to the next level."
—Richard J. Leider, Founder, The Inventure Group; author of *The Power of Purpose;* and coauthor of *Repacking Your Bags* and *Something to Live For*

"Authentic leadership lies at the intersection of our deepest spiritual values and our greatest personal gifts. Cashman's new edition of *Leadership from the Inside Out* invites you to live at this important crossroads by cultivating the habits and skills needed to enrich your professional life while fostering opportunities for rich and satisfying personal development."
—Brother Dietrich Reinhart, OSB, President, Saint John's University, Collegeville, Minnesota

"Breakthroughs in neuroscience and the plasticity of the brain directly connect to *Leadership from the Inside Out* principles and coaching model. The book gives us the tools we need for leaders to grow and develop."
—Marcelo Montero, President, Health and Nutrition, Cargill, Inc.

"*Leadership from the Inside Out* is a resource that spans the ages, integrates multiple disciplines, has experiential validity, and includes proven practical applications. Using (not just reading) this book is a transformative, peak experience."
—Robert Hayles, PhD, Consultant, QED Consulting; former Vice President of Human Resources and Diversity, Pillsbury; former Chairman of the Board, American Society for Training and Development; and coauthor of *The Diversity Directive*

"Some books are noteworthy in and of themselves. Others serve as signs that something important is happening in the world. Kevin Cashman's *Leadership from the Inside Out* meets both criteria. Throw in the fact that it is well-designed for reading and for doing the exercises throughout, and you have a real mind-opener."
—Perry Pascarella, Contributing Editor, *American Management Review*; former Editor-in-Chief, *Industry Week*; and author of *Leveraging People and Profit*

"*Leadership from the Inside Out* is full of practical inspiration and demonstrates why Kevin Cashman is regarded as a world authority on effective leadership. If you want people clamoring to be on your team, read this book!"
—David McNally, CPAE, author of *Even Eagles Need a Push* and coauthor of *Be Your Own Brand*

"With hundreds of books to choose from on the topic of leadership, it is unusual to come across one, *Leadership from the Inside Out*, that has the potential to make a meaningful change in your life."
—Larry Perlman, former Chairman and CEO, Ceridian Corporation

"Authenticity is the single most important quality of leadership. In *Leadership from the Inside Out*, Cashman not only captures the essence of inner-driven, intentional leadership, he gives both seasoned and emerging leaders a road map to navigate the challenges of personal and professional growth."
—Bob Kidder, Chairman and CEO, 3Stone Advisors LLC: former CEO, Borden Capital: and former CEO, Duracell

"*Leadership from the Inside Out* is an inspiration to lead from a deep knowledge of one's core purpose, creating value with true authenticity."
—Deborah Dunsire, MD, CEO and President, Millennium Pharmaceuticals

"The challenge of leadership is to inspire an obligation for people at all levels of an organization to step forward and lead. *Leadership from the Inside Out* gives you the practical steps to develop leaders in every nook and cranny of your organization."
—Chuck Feltz, former President and Chief Operating Officer, Lifetouch National School Studios, and former President, Deluxe Financial Services

# LEADERSHIP

## FROM THE INSIDE OUT

# LEADERSHIP
## FROM THE INSIDE OUT

*Becoming a Leader for Life*

SECOND EDITION

# KEVIN CASHMAN

Berrett–Koehler Publishers, Inc.
San Francisco
*a BK Business book*

Berrett-Koehler Publishers, Inc.
235 Montgomery Street, Suite 650
San Francisco, CA 94104-2916
Tel: (415) 288-0260      Fax: (415) 362-2512      www.bkconnection.com

**Ordering Information**
**Quantity sales.** Special discounts are available on quantity purchases by corporations, associations, and others. For details, contact the "Special Sales Department" at the Berrett-Koehler address above.
**Individual sales.** Berrett-Koehler publications are available through most bookstores. They can also be ordered directly from Berrett-Koehler: Tel: (800) 929-2929; Fax: (802) 864-7626; www.bkconnection.com
**Orders for college textbook/course adoption use.** Please contact Berrett-Koehler: Tel: (800) 929-2929; Fax: (802) 864-7626.
**Orders by U.S. trade bookstores and wholesalers.** Please contact Ingram Publisher Services, Tel: (800) 509-4887; Fax: (800) 838-1149; E-mail: customer.service@ingrampublisherservices.com; or visit www.ingrampublisherservices.com/Ordering for details about electronic ordering.

Berrett-Koehler and the BK logo are registered trademarks of Berrett-Koehler Publishers, Inc.

*Leadership from the Inside Out* is a service mark of Kevin Cashman. *Executive to Leader Institute, Chief Executive Institute, LeaderSynergy, LeaderSuccession,* and *LeaderCatalyst* are all service marks of LeaderSource, a Korn/Ferry International company. *Choices* and *Voices* are service marks of Lominger International, a Korn/Ferry International company. *Styleview* is a trademark of Decision Dynamics LLC.

Printed in the United States of America

Berrett-Koehler books are printed on long-lasting acid-free paper. When it is available, we choose paper that has been manufactured by environmentally responsible processes. These may include using trees grown in sustainable forests, incorporating recycled paper, minimizing chlorine in bleaching, or recycling the energy produced at the paper mill.

Library of Congress Cataloging-in Publication Data

Cashman, Kevin.
Leadership from the inside out: becoming a leader for life / Kevin
Cashman.—2nd ed.
p.   cm.
ISBN 978-1-57675-599-0 (pbk.: alk. paper)
1. Leadership.   2. Executives—Conduct of life.   3. Executive ability.   I. Title.

HD57.7.C373   2008
658.4'092—dc22                                        2008023639

Second Edition

13   12            10  9  8  7  6

*This book is dedicated to those value-creating leaders with the courage to commit to authentic personal transformation and the passion to serve the world around them.*

# TABLE OF CONTENTS

Breaking Free of Self-Limiting Patterns

Integrating All of Life's Experiences into a Meaningful Context

Deepening Authenticity for Sustainable Leadership

Exploring Beliefs

Reflection: Conscious Beliefs

Seven Clues That Bring Shadow Beliefs to Light

Leading with Character . . . Leading by Coping

Qualities of Character and Coping

Reflection: Character and Coping

Understanding Our Owner's Manual

Reflection: Clarifying Our Strengths and Growth Areas

Eight Points for Personal Mastery

Leadership Growth Plan: Personal Mastery

Leadership Growth Plan: Personal Mastery Example

Discovering the Sweet Spot

Identifying Core Talents

Reflection: Core Talents

Recognizing Core Values

Reflection: Core Values

Revealing Core Purpose

"Moving Upstairs" to Our Purpose

Diving Beneath the Surface to Our Purpose

Purpose Is Bigger and Deeper Than Our Goals

Connecting the Inner with the Outer: Purpose, Authenticity, and Congruence

Unfolding the Defining Thread of Purpose

Six Thousand Days

Eight Points for Purpose Mastery

Leadership Growth Plan: Purpose Mastery

## CHAPTER THREE: INTERPERSONAL MASTERY

Two Principal Streams of Leadership Development

Building Relationship Bridges

Balancing Personal Power with Synergy Power and Contribution Power

Reducing the Intention-Perception Gap

Beyond 360° Feedback to 720° Feedback

Intimate Connection of Personal Mastery and Interpersonal Mastery

Opening Up Possibilities

The Potentially Transforming Power of Presence

Moving from Leader to Opener

Trusting and Engaging in Constructive Conflict

Reflection: Building Relationships

Six Points for Authentic Interpersonal Mastery

Leadership Growth Plan: Interpersonal Mastery

## CHAPTER FOUR: CHANGE MASTERY

Uncovering the Learning and Growth Contained in Change

Breaking Old Patterns and Opening Up to Change

Developing Present-Moment Awareness to Deal with Change Effectively

Bridging the Paradox of Immediate Focus and Broad Awareness for Leading during Turbulent Times

Learning to Trust Ourselves amid Dynamic Change

Leadership Development as Measured by Our Ability to Adapt

Developing the Resilience to Thrive in Change

Change Initiatives Rarely Succeed

Seven Change Mastery Shifts

Reflection: Dealing with Change

Action Mastery Step One: Building Awareness
Reflection: Building Awareness
Action Mastery Step Two: Building Commitment
Reflection: Building Commitment
Action Mastery Step Three: Building Practice
Reflection: Building Practice
The Art of Coaching Others
Coaching Others to Build Awareness
Building Awareness in Others
Coaching Others to Build Commitment
Coaching Others to Build Practice
Parting Thoughts for Your Journey Ahead

# WHY A NEW EDITION?

It has been a decade since the original writing of *Leadership from the Inside Out*. As I step back to consider its impact, I find it very humbling and fulfilling to know that the book has been integrated into the curricula at more than 100 universities, became a number one business bestseller, and is influencing numerous leadership programs with its concepts. I ask myself, "Why did the book catch on?" Was it simply because it was one of the first leadership books to connect personal growth to leadership effectiveness? Perhaps. But, on deeper examination, I think its resonance was built on the foundation of timeless, enduring principles of human development and life effectiveness. These principles, including authenticity, courage, and purpose, are not simply values that are *nice to have*. They are enduring principles, deeply woven into the fabric of life, that produce tangible, measurable cause-and-effect relationships. They serve both parties, people on each side of the dynamic equation, and they tend to sustain their life-enriching impact for the long term. These time-tested principles are not fleeting fads, ephemeral fixes, or charm-school interventions. They are fundamental to who we are as human beings and essential to our effectiveness as leaders.

For almost 30 years, we—Korn/Ferry Leadership and Talent Consulting—have based our coaching, leadership development, and team-building practice on these same principles. Since writing the original *Leadership from the Inside Out*, it is extremely satisfying to see the mounting research from authoritative sources, which has finally caught up with and validated many of these principles. What we have known for years from working in the trenches with our clients is now being recognized and confirmed by highly credible, independent research. Jim Collins, in *Good to Great*, has validated the principles of authenticity and enduring value creation with his research on "Level 5 Leadership." John Zenger and Joseph Folkman, in *The Extraordinary Leader*, confirmed through their analysis of nearly 400,000 360° assessments that balancing people effectiveness with results orientation produces quantum leaps forward in leadership effectiveness. Daniel Goleman, in his work on emotional intelligence, clearly articulated how deepening personal awareness and interpersonal connection produces more sustainable leadership results. Lominger International and the Center for Creative Leadership's research has shown us that Learning Agility is a greater predictor of potential than raw intellectual intelligence. A study by the American Society for Training and Development (ASTD) demonstrated a 72 percent improvement in learning when coaching follows training. Korn/Ferry International and Decision Dynamics, through their *Styleview™ Decision Styles* assessment tool and study of 1.2 million leaders, have shown how effective leaders must move from task-focused decisive content to strategic and collaborative context to get to the top. It is no longer possible to discount these principles as *soft*; they produce measurable results, and they are essential to substantial leadership, team, and organizational success.

In this updated version of *Leadership from the Inside Out*, we share more of this well-founded, corroborative research, as well as our new learning. Since our last writing, we have worked with thousands of leaders in more than 60 countries. We have coached hundreds of CEOs and senior-level executives worldwide at our *Executive to Leader*® and *Chief Executive Institutes*℠. We have custom designed leadership programs for thousands more high potential leaders. We have taken scores of senior leadership groups through transformational team programs. Additionally, we have merged with Korn/Ferry International and now have 80 offices in 40 countries. We have abundant fresh perspectives to share. In the original book, we focused heavily on personal awareness and personal leadership development. While our continuing work has validated that personal awareness is essential to leadership effectiveness, it is not sufficient alone to make a lasting impact. In this edition, we go deeper and broader by expanding our coaching model with equal emphasis on Building Awareness, Building Commitment, and Building Practice, which measurably strengthens the effectiveness of your team and organization. We still hope to inspire profound moments of personal insight, but we also want to guide you into enduring, transforming practice. By the time you finish this book, our goal is for you to have had an integrated coaching and leadership development experience.

In the last several years, we have expanded and integrated our consulting practice to balance personal leadership, team leadership, and organizational leadership. At the core of these levels of leadership is the distinction we make between managers and leaders. *Managers improve what is; managers enhance what is; managers move forward what is. Leaders go beyond what is.* Indeed, if the experience of leadership is like being at the edge of an unfamiliar chasm, the act of leadership is building a bridge across that chasm. What is the bridge, then, from the known area of management to the unknown area of leadership? How do we build that bridge? This book answers those questions and offers the tools that will help you and your organization to *transcend what is*, to grow to the next level of personal, team, and organizational success.

If you have read the original *Leadership from the Inside Out*, you will find this new edition immensely enhanced by what we have learned in the marketplace during the last several years. We have integrated our dynamic leadership principles with this learning to increase their meaning and accessibility in your day-to-day leadership practices. Chapters such as Purpose Mastery, Interpersonal Mastery, Change Mastery, Resilience Mastery, and Action Mastery are even more relevant than their originals. Compelling, new stories and salient research illustrate the transformative difference coaching has made in the lives of individuals and their organizations. This book gives you a more comprehensive set of tools to apply consciously your personal, team, and organizational leadership capabilities. In fact, what we have done is create a more current representation of our principles while fostering a virtual coaching experience. I hope that once you read this book and engage in mastery of the principles and coaching practices, you will want to share it with all the leaders in your life.

# HOW TO USE THIS BOOK

## *. . . from the Inside-Out*

*Leadership from the Inside Out* guides you through a reflective journey to grow as a whole person in order to grow as a whole leader. We will not simply analyze the *external act* of leadership, breaking it down into a simplistic formula of "ten easy-to-follow" tips. However, you will gain some deep insights and practices to enhance your effectiveness as a leader for life.

You need not rush. As a matter of fact, I encourage you to set aside the urge to plow through the pages. Instead, when a thought or feeling surfaces, pause. Close the book, put up your feet, and explore the insight. If you want to capture a breakthrough, jot it down in the space provided or in your own notebook. Instead of just reading the book, experience it, digest it, and integrate it into your life.

You've probably read all sorts of personal and professional development books before; treat this one differently. Savor it as you would a walk with an old friend on a calm, sunny afternoon. There is no need to hurry, to anticipate, or to reach the end of your journey. On the contrary, your true reward is in pausing frequently and enjoying the experience itself.

On days you feel like taking a short walk, just skim the quotes. You'll find one or two that speak to your needs that day.

If you are ready to begin, let's walk together down the pathways to mastery of *Leadership from the Inside Out.*

# The Beginning of the Journey

It is a magical night—one of those rare December evenings when the cold and the warmth mix just right to blanket everything with big, fluffy, crystalline flakes of snow. Everything looks so perfect; everything feels so silent. As the snow deepens so does the silence in the atmosphere. I could be viewing this mesmerizing winter scene from a chalet in Switzerland, but I'm not. I'm in bumper-to-bumper traffic on a Minneapolis freeway, and oddly enough, I'm enjoying every minute of it.

Being in a car at rush hour can be either a prison or a monastic retreat. It all depends on your perspective. Does it really matter that I'm going to be late? Even though I could feel stressed, I don't. I could use this time to listen to messages and catch up on calls. Instead, I welcome the opportunity to sit in the quiet, and to reflect. As I sink into a meditative state, I begin to think about my day. And, what a day it was—a rich mixture of purpose, passion, emotion, and concentrated learning.

Our coaching team finished guiding a senior executive of a major company through our *Executive to Leader Institute*®. It was an intensive, rewarding three days. We helped the client master a career-life-leadership plan by integrating a comprehensive look at his professional and personal life. In a way, we helped him to step back and observe himself just as I was observing the snowfall—clearly, objectively, and appreciatively. At the end of the last session he said, "You know, I've been through all sorts of assessments, coaching, and development programs. This is the first time things have really made sense to me. I've gotten pieces of the puzzle before, but never the whole picture. I clearly understand where I'm at, where I'm headed, and what I need to do to really enhance my effectiveness. What would my organization be like if a critical mass of leaders mastered the same sense of personal conviction and clarity I have now?"

As the snow piles up, I'm feeling very fortunate. To help people connect to their purposeful potential occasionally would be lucky. But, to coach thousands of leaders, teams, and organizations for nearly 30 years and play a role in helping people and organizations to actualize their potential is deeply rewarding. I'm feeling very blessed, when suddenly I snap out of my thoughtful state and catch a glimpse of the clock. I'm an hour late! When the heck is this snow going to let up!

> *Give me beauty in the inward soul; may the outward and inward man be at one.*
>
> — Socrates

My good fortune goes beyond playing a role in the growth and development of leaders, teams, and organizations. I've learned a great deal along the way. I've had the opportunity to peek into the human dynamics supporting sustainable success, fulfillment, and effectiveness. I've learned also that these principles are not reserved for a few exceptional leaders. They are fundamental insights available to guide and to inspire us all.

> *Anyone can lead, and there is no single chief executive officer: There is a problem of getting used to the idea of no single chief, but the passage of time will allay that.*
>
> — Robert Greenleaf

While reading this book you may think, "Is this book about leadership, or is it about personal development?" It's about both. As much as we try to separate the leader from the person, the two are totally inseparable. Unfortunately, many people tend to split off the *act of leadership* from the person, team, or organization. We tend to view leadership as an external event. We only see it as something people *do*. The view of this book is different. Leadership is not simply something we do. It comes from a deeper reality within us; it comes from our values, principles, life experiences, and essence. Leadership is a process, an intimate expression of who we are. It is our whole person in action. Corey Seitz, Vice President Global Talent Management for Johnson & Johnson, shared this perspective with me: "The essence of leadership and executive development is growing the whole person to grow the whole leader. This means helping key people to connect their core values and core talents to their organization, to their customers, and to their lives. If leadership programs do that, then sustainable performance can be achieved, for leaders and for the organizations they serve."

*We lead by virtue of who we are.* Some people reading this book will make breakthroughs and then lead their own lives more effectively. Others will develop themselves and passionately lead major organizations to new heights. Whether we are at an early stage in our career, a mid-level manager, or a senior executive, we are all CEOs of our own lives. The only difference is the domain of influence. The process is the same; we lead from who we are. The leader and the person are one. As we learn to master our growth as a person, we will be on the path to mastery of *Leadership from the Inside Out*.

What does *mastery* of leadership mean to you? To many people it is mastery *of* something: mastery *of* the skill to be a dynamic public speaker, mastery *of* strategic planning and visioning, mastery *of* consistent achievements and results. Instead of being seen as an ongoing, internal growth process, mastery is usually seen as mastery *of* something outside of ourselves. When you think about it, it's no wonder that our ideas about mastery and leadership tend to be externalized. Our training, development, and educational systems focus on learning about *things*. We learn *what* to think, not *how* to think. We learn *what* to do, not *how* to be. We learn *what* to achieve, not *how* to achieve. We learn about *things*, not the *nature of things*. We tend to fill up the container of knowledge but rarely consider comprehending it, expanding it, or using it more effectively. In organizations, this external pattern continues. As leaders of organizations and communities, we receive recognition for our external mastery. Our success is measured by the degree to which we have mastered our external environment. Revenue, profit, new product breakthroughs, cost savings, and market share are only some of the measures of our external competencies. Few would question the value of achieving and measuring external results. That isn't the real issue. The core questions are: Where do the external results come from? Is focusing on external achievement the sole source of greater accomplishment? Could it be that our single-minded focus on external results is causing us to miss the underlying dynamics supporting sustainable peak performance? Malcolm Forbes said, "Only a handful of companies understand that all successful business operations come down to three basic principles: People, Product, Profit. Without TOP people, you cannot do much with the others."

Our definitions of leadership also tend to be externalized. Most descriptions of leadership focus on the *outer manifestations* of leadership (i.e., vision, innovation, results, drive, etc.), instead of getting to the fundamental, *essence of leadership* itself. For years, many companies came to us with their beautiful leadership models. One day I had a meeting with representatives from one of these companies. When they walked into my office, I noticed that they were carrying an imposing, massive document. They dropped it onto my desk with a thud. When I asked them what it was, they said with obvious pride, "This is our leadership competency model." A bit taken aback by its size, I said, "Gee, it looks pretty big. How many competencies are in there?" With a knowing confidence, they said, "Eighty-four." Not sure how to respond to this, but wanting to provoke their thinking, I asked, "Have you ever met one?" The certainty in their eyes disappeared. Their faces twisted into puzzlement, and they asked, "What do you mean?" I explained. "In the whole history of civilization have you ever met anyone who has all these qualities at all times in all circumstances? In your organization have you ever met anyone with all these qualities?" They said that they hadn't, and I pressed further. "But you want everybody to have all 84 competencies all the time, right?" We went

> *The essence of leadership is not giving things or even providing visions. It is offering oneself and one's spirit.*
>
> — Lee Bolman and Terrance Deal

back and forth like this until finally I made my point. Companies create perfection myths about what they want or expect of leaders. Although aspiring to all those competencies may be noble, it also would be unrealistic to find all of them embodied in a real person.

We are not saying that we do not support competency models. In fact, we help companies globally build leadership competency models directly correlated to their business strategies. But when competency models are perfectionist, mythical, and unconnected to the business needs, they are counterproductive.

As a result of seeing too many of these mythical competency models, we decided to step back and look at the most effective clients that we had coached over the last 30 years. After reviewing thousands of personality assessments and 360° assessments, we challenged ourselves with the question, "What is fundamental to the most effective, results-producing leaders that supports their various competencies or styles?" Three patterns became clear:

1. *Authenticity:* Well-developed self-awareness that openly faces strengths, vulnerabilities, and development challenges.
2. *Influence:* Meaningful communication that connects with people by reminding self and others what is genuinely important.
3. *Value Creation:* Passion and aspiration to serve multiple constituencies—self, team, organization, world, family, community—to sustain performance and contribution over the long term.

Continuing to evaluate and test these emerging principles over the next 18 months, we landed on what we think is an essential definition of personal leadership:

**Leadership is authentic influence that creates value.**

The implications of this definition are potentially far-reaching. From this new perspective, leadership is not viewed as hierarchical; it exists everywhere in organizations. The roles of leadership change, but the core process is the same. Anyone who is authentically influencing to create value is leading. Some may influence and create value through ideas, others through systems, yet others through people, but the essence is the same. Deep from their core, leaders bring forward their talents, connect with others, and serve multiple constituencies.

Reacting to this definition of leadership, John Hetterick, former President of Tonka and CEO of Rollerblade, told me, "This definition of leadership speaks to me. The single biggest performance issue organizations face is inspiring leadership at all levels."

Using this definition, we acknowledge that there are an infinite number of ways to manifest leadership. There are as many styles of leadership as there are leaders. Viewing leadership from this vantage point, we will be exploring three essential questions to enhance our leadership effectiveness:

- How can we enhance our *authenticity* as a leader?
- How can we extend the *influence* we have?
- How can we create more *value*?

*Leadership from the Inside Out* is about our ongoing journey to discover and develop our purposeful inner capabilities to make a more positive contribution to the world around us. Bill George, former Chairman and CEO of Medtronic, shares this view: "As leaders, the more we can unleash our whole capabilities—mind, body, spirit—the more value we can create within and outside of our organizations."

Mastery of *Leadership from the Inside Out* is not merely a function of achieving things. It is principally about achieving one thing—consciously making a difference by fully applying more of our potential. This does not mean that we only lead from the inside-out. On the contrary, we lead just as much—and sometimes more—from the outside-in. Leadership involves a constant dynamic between the inner and the outer. We are emphasizing the inside-out dynamic because too often it is overlooked. We tend to focus too much on the outside. We are in a continuing flow, a dynamic relationship with ourselves and our constituencies—the marketplace, our customers, our employees, and our personal relationships. Ultimately, we want a balance of leading from the inside-out and the outside-in. Our decisions and actions are in a dynamic loop from us to others and back again. To practice leadership at the highest level, we need to take responsibility—personal and social responsibility. We need to be equally vigilant about the "I" and the "We" of effective leadership. Daniel Goleman's work on emotional intelligence precisely identified this inner-outer/outer-inner dynamic as the two interactive qualities of emotional intelligence: awareness of self and awareness of others.

> *There is but one cause of human failure and that is a man's lack of faith in his true Self.*
>
> — William James

The purpose of this book is to help you master seven ways to lead more effectively. I will do this by sharing our* distilled insights from working with thousands of leaders. Although the subsequent chapters will elaborate, there are a few essential themes, which consistently surface as we help people to master their leadership effectiveness:

- As the person grows, the leader grows. The missing element in most leadership development programs is actually the "Master Competency" of *growing the whole person to grow the whole leader.*
- Most definitions of leadership need to be balanced from the inside-out, moving from viewing leadership only in terms of its external manifestations to seeing it also from its internal source. To balance leading from the inside-out and from the outside-in gets to the essence of genuine leadership development.
- Helping leaders to connect with their core talents, core values, and core beliefs is central to effective leadership development.
- Leaders who learn to bring their core talents, core values, and core purpose to conscious awareness experience dramatic, quantum increases in energy and effectiveness.
- Leaders who integrate personal power and results power with relational power accelerate their leadership effectiveness.
- Leaders who work on achieving congruence—alignment of their real values and their actions—are more energetic, resilient, effective, and interpersonally connected.
- Transforming leadership development programs from a series of fragmented, content-driven events to an integrated, inside-out/outside-in growth process greatly enhances leadership, team, and organizational excellence.

Kevin Wilde, Chief Learning Officer for General Mills, who was named "CLO of the Year" by *Chief Learning Officer* magazine, put it this way, "Ultimately, leadership development has to integrate the depth of the inner self-awareness work with the breadth and complexity of external marketplace and cultural dynamics. Enduring leadership development brings together both of these inner and outer realities."

---

* Since much of the work we do at Korn/Ferry Leadership and Talent Consulting and the *Executive to Leader Institute* involves integrated teams of coaches working together to impact individual and organizational effectiveness, I cannot accurately write about the work without saying "our," "we," and so forth.

*Leadership from the Inside Out* involves clarifying our inner identity, purpose, and vision so that our lives thereafter are dedicated to a more conscious, intentional manner of living and leading. This inner mastery directs our diverse intentions and aspirations into a purposeful focus where increased effectiveness is a natural result. As we move to a more fulfilled manner of living and leading, a focus on purpose replaces our single-minded focus on external success. However, our purpose cannot stay "bottled up" inside; we feel compelled to express it. This purposeful intention and action serves as the energetic, inspired basis for enhanced leadership effectiveness and achievement. Unfortunately, I've lost track of the number of times I've met with a CEO, business owner, or corporate executive who had lost connection to this inner core of success.

John, a business owner, approached me a while ago. By all external measures he was a great success. He had a thriving business. He recently built a new facility to house his expanding operations. But something was missing. When he sat down with me, he opened up immediately by saying, "You know, everyone thinks I'm a big success. My neighbors think I'm successful. My friends think I'm successful. My family thinks I'm successful. My employees around the globe think I have it all together. But you know what? I'm miserable. I'm unhappy in what I'm doing. *My whole life I've been just successfully reacting to circumstances.* I got my degree and that defined my first job, and that first job defined my second job, and so on. And before I knew it I had this business, a family, and a mortgage. Recently I 'woke up' and said to myself, 'Is this me? Is this my life, or just a series of circumstances I've successfully reacted to?' I'm not sure what to do, but I have this sense of urgency that I need to take my life back."

From a development perspective, many leaders of organizations today are like John. We are like naturally gifted athletes who have mastered our external performance capabilities but have neglected the inner dynamics supporting our success and fulfillment. What happens to natural athletes who become coaches? They often have an extremely difficult and frustrating time. Why? Most often it is because they have not comprehended from the inside-out how they became great. As a result, it is challenging to mentor others to greatness, and it is equally challenging to be consciously aware of how to replicate their own success in the future. This is why most significant growth and development needs to begin with self-leadership, mastery of oneself.

When we define our identity and purpose only in terms of external results, the circumstances of our lives define us. In this externally driven state of identity, life is fragile, vulnerable, and at risk. Everything that happens to us defines who we are. We are success. We are failure. We become our circumstances. Life defines us. Our core identity and passionate

> *Try not to become a man of success. Try to become a man of value.*
>
> — Albert Einstein

purpose are overshadowed by the events of our lives. Success may even be present, but mastery has escaped us. Unintentionally, we have chosen to "major" in the "minor" things of life. Can we lead when we don't see beyond the external circumstances surrounding us?

Bill, a senior executive in a global company based in Europe, was caught in this external trap, but he didn't know it. His career had been a fast and consistent ascent to the top. He had the "right degree," his background was with the "right companies," and his results were always outstanding. However, his single-minded

> *For this is the journey that men make: to find themselves. If they fail to do this, it doesn't matter much what else they find.*
>
> — James Michener

pursuit of success had great costs. Without intending to, he left a wide wake of people in his path to success. As a result, he had few close supporters and team morale was low. At earlier stages in his career, this was not an issue. As he advanced, it became an increasing problem. One day his boss approached him and said, "Bill, your results are outstanding, but we need more than that. The way you're getting results is starting to diminish your effectiveness here." Bill was shocked. A flood of thoughts came to mind: "What do you mean my results are not enough? Since when has my style been an issue?" Am I missing something here?" Bill's externally built facade of success was being questioned by his boss and by Bill himself. This jolt was exactly what he needed to foster his development to the next level.

After a few days, Bill arrived in my office for leadership coaching. The shock of his boss's comments and his need to reconcile them with his limited self-understanding had put him in a reflective mood. "I've been avoiding this. If I'm honest with myself, I know I have to do some work. Not the type of work I'm accustomed to, but work on me. But I'm totally at a loss. My whole life has been focused on achieving at all costs: getting the grades in school, winning in sports, getting results in business. When I'm faced with changing, doing things differently, growing . . . whatever you call it, I'm lost. I'm even beginning to wonder what's really important to me anymore. My life has been invested in getting results. Now that's not enough? What do I do?"

After a couple of months of intensive work, Bill began to turn his life inside-out. He started to sort out what was really important to him. He began leading more from his core values.

He built more relationships with people. He started to master the power of inner-driven, purposeful leadership. His team environment responded to his newfound sense of service. His boss, co-workers, friends, and family all felt that something significant, something of real substance, had begun.

It's important to note that we didn't try to change Bill by taking him through some sort of "charm school." We helped him to wake up. He woke up to his identity. He woke up to the influence he was having on people. He woke up to his values and purpose. He woke up to his vision. He woke up to how others perceived him. This inside-out and outside-in mastery authentically reconnected him to himself, to others, and to the world around him. It was there all the time, but he needed to connect to it. Like Bill, we all fall into a metaphorical slumber at times. Rarely questioning where we are going and why, we go about our business and relationships day after day. Unfortunately, it often takes a traumatic event—a death, a termination, a divorce, a disease, or even a global crisis—to bring us out of the depths of our deep sleep. But why wait for a shocking wake-up call? Why not make a more conscious choice to awaken to new potentialities now?

# REFLECTION

## CONSCIOUS WAKE-UP CALL

Go to your favorite spot to sit. Get comfortable. Close your eyes but don't lie down. (Remember, this is an awakening exercise, so our goal is to wake up, not to sleep!) Listen to your internal dialogue and chatter: "This is a dumb exercise!" "Why did I buy this book?" "I'm hungry." "I'm tired." "I'm worried about . . ." Observe the dialogue in a non-judging way. Don't mind your thoughts and feelings; just let them be there and pass in and out. Let your thoughts settle down. This will happen naturally in your non-judging state.

Start to listen. Listen for your inner voice, not the one in your head with the dialogue and thoughts. Listen for the one in your gut, the impulse that speaks to you through feelings, inspirations, intuitions, and possibilities.

From that place, ask questions and listen: "What is really important to me? Is this the life I want to live? How do I really want to live my life? What gives passion, meaning, and purpose to my life? How can I make even more of a difference? How can I live connected to these inner values?" Pause deeply. Let the questions and answers come to you easily and spontaneously.

Some people prefer doing this while listening to gentle music, others while walking; there are many ways to open up to this state. Use whatever way works for you and practice it regularly. There are endless layers to explore. If you're a bit uncomfortable or embarrassed at first, don't worry about it. Over time you will settle into it, and your discomfort will pass.

When was the last time you woke up in the morning feeling thankful, fulfilled, and happy to be alive? On these days, the sun seemed brighter, your sense of self stronger, your life's purpose clearer, and your mental and physical energies more abundant. These moments did not happen by accident. Several aspects of your life "came together." Your self-recognition, sense of purpose, relationships, career, health, and lifestyle were all "more alive" at these times. As a result, you found yourself thinking, feeling, leading, and achieving in a more positive and energizing way.

For at least a brief period of time, each of us experiences these masterful moments. How can we experience them on a more consistent basis? Unfortunately, there is not a simple answer. There are no quick-fix programs in leadership development. Programs that take shortcuts may get some immediate results by temporarily masking acute symptoms, but the chronic situation remains. Over time, the person returns to an even more difficult condition. "Quick fixes" may be quick, but they don't fix anything. The people I've worked with over the years are looking for something more—mastery of excellence over the long haul.

These people are not interested in getting "psyched-up" by a motivational speaker; they are interested in substance, results, process, and research-based solutions. They want to reach a deeper, more comprehensive level to master their lives as a whole.

Knowingly or unknowingly, we attempt to master personal and professional situations according to how we *interpret* our experiences. We filter our experiences through our unique belief system and create our personal reality. For instance, if we were in a totally dark room, we could attempt to gain mastery by interpreting it in a variety of ways:

- We could curse the darkness and become very effective at blaming it for all our problems;
- We could struggle and strain, trying with all our might to force the darkness out of the room;
- We could accept the darkness as a natural part of our existence and even create an elaborate belief system around our particular dark experience;
- We could pretend the darkness does not exist and maybe even convince ourselves that the room is actually full of light;
- Or we could take the advice of people who have been in this room before: "Turn on the light switch and dispel the darkness."

*Leadership from the Inside Out* is about lighting the pathways to our growth and development. It is not about ignoring negativity, convincing ourselves it does not exist, or pretend-

> *Only that day dawns to which we are awake.*
> — Henry David Thoreau

ing things are fine when they are not. Joseph Campbell, in *The Power of Myth,* described how effective, heroic people acknowledged and faced both the darkness and the light. They learned to acknowledge both realities as part of the whole. But, as Campbell emphasized, "Although they stand at the neutral point between darkness and light, they always leaned into the light." *Leadership from the Inside Out* will help you to face your toughest challenges and lean into the light.

After years of helping leaders and teams to enhance career, life, and organizational effectiveness, we have identified seven practices for mastery of *Leadership from the Inside Out.* These practices are not stages of development arranged in a sequential or hierarchical order. Rather, they are an ongoing, interrelated growth process in which the practices are illuminating one another. When arranged together, we can think of them as an integrated whole, with each practice supporting progress toward a more fulfilling destination: making an enduring difference from within.

Now it's time to begin our journey. Each of the following chapters offers you pragmatic torches to illuminate your pathways to *Leadership from the Inside Out.*

# CHAPTER ONE

# PERSONAL MASTERY

## *Leading with Awareness and Authenticity*

I once heard a poignant story about a priest who was confronted by a soldier while he was walking down a road in pre-revolutionary Russia. The soldier, aiming his rifle at the priest, commanded, "Who are you? Where are you going? Why are you going there?" Unfazed, the priest calmly replied, "How much do they pay you?" Somewhat surprised, the soldier responded, "Twenty-five kopecks a month." The priest paused, and in a deeply thoughtful manner said, "I have a proposal for you. I'll pay you fifty kopecks each month if you stop me here every day and challenge me to respond to those same three questions."

How many of us have a "soldier" confronting us with life's tough questions, pushing us to pause, to examine, and to develop ourselves more thoroughly? If "character is our fate," as Heraclitus wrote, do we step back often enough both to question and to affirm ourselves in order to reveal our character? As we lead others and ourselves through tough times, do we draw on the inner resources of our character, or do we lose ourselves in the pressures of the situation?

## BREAKING FREE OF SELF-LIMITING PATTERNS

Joe Cavanaugh, Founder and CEO of Youth Frontiers, in one of his powerful retreats on character development, tells a moving story about Peter, an elementary school student who suffered burns on 90 percent of his body. Peter's burns were so severe that his mouth had to be propped open so it wouldn't seal shut in the healing process. Splints separated his fingers so his hands wouldn't become webbed. His eyes were kept open so his eyelids wouldn't cut him off from the world permanently. Even after Peter endured one year of rehabilitation and excruciating pain, his spirit was intact. What was the first thing he did when he could walk? He helped console all the other patients by telling them that they would be all right, that they would get through it. His body may have been horribly burned, but his strength of character was whole.

Eventually, Peter had to begin junior high at a school where no one knew him. Imagine going to a new school at that age and being horribly disfigured. Imagine what the other kids

*Courage is the ladder on which all other virtues mount.*

— Claire Booth Luce

would say and how they would react. On his first day in the cafeteria everyone avoided him. They looked at him with horror and whispered to one another. Kids got up and moved from tables that were close to him. One student, Laura, had the courage to approach him and to introduce herself. As they talked and ate, she looked into Peter's eyes and sensed the person beneath the scarred surface. Reading her thoughts, Peter, in his deep, raspy, smoke-damaged voice, said, "Everyone is avoiding me because they don't know me yet. When they come to know me, they'll hang out with me. When they get to know the real me inside, they'll be my friends." Peter was right. His character was so strong that people eventually looked beyond the surface. People loved his spirit and wanted to be his friend.

When I consider Peter's situation, I'm not so sure that I would be able to come through his experiences with the same courage. But that's the beauty of Personal Mastery. Peter was challenged to awaken his extraordinary strength and to walk down his particular path. It was his path to master, not yours, not mine. Somehow his life had prepared him to walk that path with dignity. Although usually under less dramatic conditions than Peter's, each of us is challenged to master our own unique circumstances. *Each of us is being called to lead by authentically connecting our own life experiences, values, and talents to the special circumstances we face.* Our ability to rise to the challenge depends on our understanding of our gifts, as well as how prepared we are to take the journey with grace and contribution.

## INTEGRATING ALL OF LIFE'S EXPERIENCES INTO A MEANINGFUL CONTEXT

Personal Mastery is not a simplistic process of merely affirming our strengths while ignoring our weaknesses. It is, as Carl Jung would explain it, *"growth toward wholeness."* It is about acknowledging our talents and strengths while facing our underdeveloped, hidden, or shadow sides of ourselves. It is about honestly facing and reconciling all facets of self. Personal Mastery involves appreciating the rich mixture of our life experiences and how they dynamically form our unique existence. Peter Senge, in *The Fifth Discipline,* wrote, "People with a high level of personal mastery are acutely aware of their ignorance, their incompetence, their growth areas, and they are deeply self-confident. Paradoxical? Only for those who do not see the journey is the reward."

*There is nothing noble in being superior to your fellow men, true nobility is being superior to your former self.*

— Lao Tzu

Research by Lominger International, a Korn/Ferry Company, indicates that defensiveness, arrogance, overdependence on a single skill, key skill deficiencies, lack of composure, and unwillingness to adapt to differences are among the "top ten career stallers and stoppers." A research study by Kenneth Brousseau, CEO of Decision Dynamics, Gary Hourihan, Chairman of Korn/Ferry's consulting division, and others, published in the February 2006 edition of the *Harvard Business Review*, connects the significance of personal growth—an evolving decision-making and leadership style—to leadership and career advancement. This global research, with its extraordinarily high degree of statistical credibility, which used the *Styleview*$^{tm}$ *Decision Styles* assessment tool on 180,000 individuals in five levels of management from entry level to the top, shows that if people don't develop, they do not advance.

## DEEPENING AUTHENTICITY FOR SUSTAINABLE LEADERSHIP

Of all the principles supporting sustainable leadership, authenticity may be the most important. It also can be the most challenging. Most people never realize that it's an area of their lives that needs attention. In almost three decades of interacting with thousands of leaders, I've yet to meet an executive for coaching who comes to me lamenting, "I'm having real trouble being authentic." If authenticity is so important, why don't we recognize it as an issue? The answer is both simple and profound: *We are always authentic to our present state of development.* We all behave in perfect alignment with our current level of emotional, psychological, and spiritual evolution. All our actions and relationships, as well as the quality and power of our leadership, accurately express the person we have become. Therefore, we conclude that we are "authentic," because we are doing the best we can with the information and experience that we have at this time.

There is a big hitch, however. While we are true and authentic to our current state of development, *we are inauthentic to our potential state of development.* As Shakespeare wrote so eloquently in *Hamlet*, "We know what we are, but not what we may be." As humans and as leaders, we have an infinite ability to grow, to be and to become more. Our horizons are unlimited. If there is an end-point to growing in authenticity, I certainly have not seen it. In *The Developing Mind: How Relationships and the Brain Interact to Shape Who We Are*, Daniel J. Siegel explains that the mind is shaped continually throughout life by the connection between the neurophysiological processes of the brain and interpersonal relationships. "When we examine what is known about how the mind develops, we can gain

*Dig inside. Inside is the fountain of good and it will forever flow if you will forever dig.*

— Marcus Aurelius

important insights into the ways in which people can continue to grow throughout life." He goes on to say, "We can use an understanding of the impact of experience on the mind to deepen our grasp of how the past continues to shape present experience and influence future actions."

To deepen authenticity, to nourish leadership from the inside-out, takes time and attention. In today's world, the amount of distraction and busyness we all experience keeps us from undertaking the inward journey and engaging in the quiet reflection required to become more authentic human beings. By middle life, most of us are accomplished fugitives from ourselves. John Gardener writes:

> Human beings have always employed an enormous variety of clever devices for running away from themselves. We can keep ourselves so busy, fill our lives with so many diversions, stuff our heads with so much knowledge, involve ourselves with so many people and cover so much ground that we never have time to probe the fearful and wonderful world within.

To penetrate the commotion and distraction of our lives, to explore the depths of ourselves is the prerequisite for self-awareness and authenticity. So what is authenticity? Based on our experience coaching leaders over the years, we define authenticity as the continual process of building self-awareness of our whole person—strengths and limitations. As a result of this awareness, more often than not, the authentic person's beliefs, values, principles, and behavior tend to line up. Commonly referred to as "walking the talk," authenticity also means being your talk at a very deep level.

Another prominent feature of highly authentic individuals is openness. Whether they come to authenticity naturally or work hard to attain it, the most real, genuine, sincere people tend to be open to both their capabilities and their vulnerabilities. They have an inner openness with themselves about their strengths as well as their limitations. They know who they are and don't apologize for their capabilities. They also have an outer openness with others about their whole selves. They try neither to cover up their weaknesses nor to "hide their light under a bushel." They have managed to avoid the pitfall that Malcolm Forbes elucidates, "Too many people over-value what they are not and under-value what they are." Self-compassion, being open and receptive to our vulnerabilities, is an important aspect of authenticity. By acknowledging our own vulnerabilities and appreciating our whole selves, we can truly be compassionate to others. As David Whyte, poet and author of *The Heart Aroused*, has written, "We need to learn to love that part of ourselves that limps."

In *Good to Great: Why Some Companies Make the Leap . . . and Others Don't*, Jim Collins' research points out the interesting duality in "Level 5 Leaders," who were both modest and willful, humble and fearless, vulnerable and strong, interpersonally connected and focused—in short, leaders we would say "had grown toward wholeness" and authenticity. Their "compelling modesty," as Collins puts it, their authenticity as we would term it, draws people to come together to achieve.

Authentic people—people on the path to personal mastery—value all of who they are. A dual awareness of their own strengths and vulnerabilities allows authentic leaders to focus on the team, organization, and marketplaces, not on themselves. Personal Mastery allows us to transcend our egos and move into authentic service and authentic contribution. As Collins elaborates, "Level 5 leaders channel their ego away from themselves and into the larger goal of building a great company. It's not that Level 5 Leaders have no ego or self-interest. Indeed they are incredibly ambitious, but their ambition is first and foremost for the contribution, not for themselves." Level 5 Leaders—authentic leaders—see their purpose beyond their limited selves as passionate instruments of service and contribution. Authentic leaders understand that if our lives do not stand for something bigger than ourselves, our leadership lacks purpose. Deepak Chopra wrote:

> To be authentic, you have to be everything that you are, omitting nothing. Within everyone there is light and shadow, good and evil, love and hate. The play of these opposites is what constantly moves life forward; the river of life expresses itself in all its changes from one opposite to another. As we discover and accept these opposites within ourselves, we are being more authentic.

In Daniel Goleman's extensive research on emotional intelligence in the workplace, Goleman cites self-awareness, "attention to one's own experience or mindfulness," as the primary competence in his framework for managing ourselves, a prerequisite for managing others. In *Primal Leadership: Learning to Lead with Emotional Intelligence*, he and his co-authors, Richard Boyatzis and Annie McKee, assert, "A leader's self-awareness and ability to accurately perceive his performance is as important as the feedback he receives from others." The flow of crucial information comes from the inside-out and from the outside-in.

> *What you bring forth out of yourself from the inside will save you. What you do not bring forth out of yourself from the inside will destroy you.*
>
> — Gospel of Thomas

Although the world may be headed toward a time when top-down, authoritarian leadership will be outmoded, I have seen authoritarian leaders with substantial authenticity out-perform leaders who strove to be collaborative, yet lacked authenticity. I've seen leaders low in charisma and polish get in front of a group and stumble around a bit, but their personal authenticity and substance were so tangibly established that they inspired the group members and moved them to a new level of excellence. Could such leaders benefit from working on their style of presentation? Certainly. But how much would it really matter, compared with their trust-inspiring authenticity? "The individual who does not embody her messages will eventually be found out," warns Howard Gardner in *Leading Minds*. "Even the inarticulate individual who leads the exemplary life may eventually come to be appreciated."

## EXPLORING BELIEFS

One of the most effective ways to take this journey to a more integrated, complete understanding of ourselves is to explore deeply our personal belief system. Few psychological dynamics are as fundamental as our beliefs. Beliefs literally create our reality; they are the lenses or filters through which we interpret the world. Some of these "lenses" focus and open up new horizons; others dim our view and limit possibilities. Beliefs are transformational. Every belief we have transforms our life in either a life-enriching or life-limiting way.

One of the most dramatic examples of the transformational power of beliefs comes from heavyweight fighter George Foreman. In the 1970s, Foreman was renowned for being one of the toughest, nastiest human beings on the planet. Angry and antisocial, he often came across as a tough, mean, uncommunicative person, not at all the person you see today. He was not known for social graces, self-awareness, or his big smile. Immediately following his surprising loss to Jimmy Young in Puerto Rico, George went to his dressing room, lay down on the training table, and reportedly had an overwhelming spiritual experience. After that experience, George changed. He changed his entire life, everything: his personality, his relationships, his life purpose. He transformed them all into a more life-affirming direction.

George peeled the onion of his personality and the delightful, humorous, self-effacing "George" came forward. The important thing to note here is not whether George Foreman actually had a spiritual revelation. Many medical professionals said he suffered from severe heat exhaustion, and that's what caused his "experience." That's not the issue. The key principle is that George Foreman believed he had a spiritual transformation and the belief changed his life. What we believe, we become.

Through my years of coaching people, I have observed consistently two distinct types of belief systems operating in people: *Conscious Beliefs* and *Shadow Beliefs*. Conscious Beliefs are the explicit, known beliefs we have. When asked about these beliefs about ourselves, about other people, or about life in general, we can articulate many of them. Even though it may take some effort to access and to clarify some of these beliefs, they are accessible to us on an everyday level. Examples of Conscious Beliefs someone might have are: "I believe in treating people with respect; I fear trying new things; I am creative and resilient; many people are untrustworthy; hard work brings results." Although we can access these beliefs on a conscious level, this does not mean we are always aware of them. We can, however, become more aware of Conscious Beliefs and whether or not we are living in accordance with these beliefs.

Recently, we guided the chairman of the board of a fast-growing public company through the process of bringing his beliefs into conscious awareness. As a result, the 60-year-old chairman remarked, "Most people probably think I had this all figured out. What I discovered is that my beliefs were operating, but not consciously enough. After more than 30 years in leadership roles, I realize that unknowingly I've been holding back crucial aspects of myself, critical to continued leadership success. Once I saw it in my work, it was easy to see that I was doing the same thing at home with my family."

Elena was an executive in a global service firm in the United Kingdom. Her intelligence, energetic work ethic, results orientation, and excellent relationship skills had supported her pattern of success. She prided herself on how connected the people on her team were with her and each other. In meetings, team members conducted themselves respectfully, and they rarely engaged in conflict. One day during a one-on-one with her boss, Elena was taken aback when her boss said, "Elena, you've been on the team for a while now, and you never disagree with me. I don't really know if you are really invested in all these new changes we're making, or if you are just going along with them. You're too nice! I need you to step forward more powerfully and challenge me." Ingrained in Elena from a young age was the fear of rejection, which operated with the belief that being liked and accepted was the only way to really connect with people. Elena's boss encouraged her to see that speaking up, being more open, is not only more

> *To leave our self-defeating behaviors behind, we must use our conscious minds to undermine the destructive but unconscious beliefs that cause us to defeat ourselves.*
> — Milton Cudney and Robert Hardy

respectful but also more authentic. After working with Elena for a while, we were able to help her break free of Shadow Beliefs around rejection and see that fostering more open discussions, even constructive conflict, surfaces not only unspoken issues but also innovation. As we believe, so shall we lead.

Although we access Conscious Beliefs somewhat easily, Shadow Beliefs are subtler and much more challenging to uncover. Doing so, however, is crucial to high performance. Taken from the Jungian concept of shadow, Shadow Beliefs are those beliefs that are manifestations of hidden, unexplored, or unresolved psychological dynamics. A Shadow Belief is cast when we don't want to deal with something. When we hold onto a type of "secret," a lack of awareness, we hold onto a Shadow Belief within us.

> *Personality can open doors. Only character can keep them open.*
> — Elmer Letterman

We all have Shadow Beliefs. If we don't think we do, then the shadow is probably operating at precisely that moment by obscuring a view of a portion of ourselves. Jeffrey Patnaude, in his work *Leading from the Maze*, writes, "The leader must be awake and fully alert. Like a nighttime traveler attuned to every sound in the forest, the leader must be aware of all possibilities lurking in the shadows. For we can neither challenge nor transform what we cannot see."

On a personal level, some of my Shadow Beliefs have to do with exceptionally high standards for others and myself. From a young age, I evaluated myself by this external, often critical, yardstick. As a result, I developed a series of Shadow Beliefs: "I'm never quite good enough; I have to work twice as hard to be valued; if something is not exceptional, it is not worthwhile; I am afraid to fail." As you can see, these beliefs have some value. They have fueled a drive to achieve. On the other hand, some of these same beliefs cast a shadow on my behavior and relationships at times. However, when I am actively committed to fostering my awareness of these shadows, I've been able to shed some light on them and hopefully minimize their limiting influence on others and me.

Transforming Shadow Beliefs to Conscious Beliefs is crucial to Personal Mastery. This is not to say we don't struggle continually with them. We do. The difference is we consciously engage them vs. unconsciously being driven by them. What happens to us if we don't deal with Shadow Beliefs? We pay a high price. Addictive behaviors, difficulty in relationships, achievement overdrive, imbalanced lifestyles, and health problems can be some of the costs associated with them. Shadow Beliefs are not scary; not dealing with them is.

While I was coaching Steven, the president of a multibillion-dollar international firm based in Latin America, a Shadow Belief that was limiting him surfaced. Let me preface this story by explaining that Steven was not referred to us because he had any "issues." He was wildly successful in his current role. His consumer products firm was number one in revenue and market share globally for four consecutive years. In fact, it was his success that was starting to be a problem for him. He had this nagging anxiety—"Can I continue to top my past achievements?" Each time we would explore future plans, he would conjure up all sorts of disaster scenarios. As I got to know him better, I understood that he had internalized a hidden belief that no matter how hard he worked or what he achieved, it could all go away tomorrow. On one level this Shadow Belief served him well; it gave him the drive to achieve many goals. However, because he wasn't aware of it, his fear of failure was actually inhibiting him from risking new experiences and new learning. It also was squeezing the life out of his team, which was totally inconsistent with his values and intentions. Finally I asked Steven, "You don't get it, do you?" Surprised, he looked at me and said, "Get what?" I responded, "Steven, look at your life. You succeed in all areas of your life: your career, your family, your relationships. What evidence do you have that you are going to fail at your next endeavor?" It was a defining moment for Steven. He saw the shadow and brought it into the light. He moved from trusting his fear to trusting his contributions. He brought a Shadow Belief into the Conscious Belief arena. Before that moment he wasn't aware of its presence. It had been controlling him, and now he was beginning to take control of it. A few months later, describing his experience, he said, "This one insight has opened a doorway for me. It has given me the peace of mind to trust myself and to lead from who I am. I now know that no matter what I attempt, I will make it a success, and if not, I will adapt, learn, and somehow make it work."

# REFLECTION

## CONSCIOUS BELIEFS

Take a few minutes to explore some of your Conscious Beliefs—the self-conversations we have that reveal what we hold to be true, important, and of value.

- What do you believe about yourself?

- What do you believe about other people?

- What do you believe about your teams?

- What do you believe about life?

- What do you believe is your impact or influence on others?

- What do you believe about leadership?

## SEVEN CLUES THAT BRING SHADOW BELIEFS TO LIGHT

How often have you heard the expression that "an overdeveloped strength can become a weakness"? Although there is truth to this statement, there is also a deeper underlying dynamic. Why do some strengths turn into weaknesses? Usually because some Shadow Belief is operating. Leaders either shed light or cast a shadow on everything they do. The more conscious the self-awareness, the more light leaders bring. The more limited the self-understanding, the bigger the shadow a leader casts. Let's say we have a Shadow Belief that "we only have value if we are doing and achieving." If we are unaware of this Shadow Belief, our drive and determination will soon turn into workaholism and lack of intimacy, with profound negative implications for our health and relationships. Let's say we have intelligence and self-confidence as strengths combined with a Shadow Belief that "we always have to be right." Without sufficient awareness, our self-confidence will turn into arrogance, abrasiveness, and self-righteousness. Here are some other examples of how shadows can potentially turn strengths into weaknesses:

*The ideal is in thyself; the impediment, too, is in thyself.*
— Thomas Carlyle

| STRENGTH | + | SHADOW BELIEF | = | WEAKNESS |
|---|---|---|---|---|
| Energy | | "I can never give up." | | Mania |
| Charm | | "I must succeed no matter what." | | Manipulation |
| Conscientiousness | | "I can always do better." | | Compulsiveness |
| Focus | | "I must know every detail to feel comfortable." | | Rigidity/Lack of Trust |
| Courage | | "I must always achieve more." | | Foolhardiness |
| Presence | | "I must always be seen as exceptional." | | Narcissism/Self-Focus |

Since our shadows are often hidden successfully from our own view, how can we bring them to light? Over the years, we've developed seven clues to indicate if a shadow may be operating:

- *Shadow Clue One:* If other people often give us feedback inconsistent with how we see ourselves, a shadow is present.
- *Shadow Clue Two:* When we feel stuck or blocked with a real loss as to what to do next, a shadow is holding us back.
- *Shadow Clue Three:* As strengths become counterproductive, some hidden dynamics need to surface.
- *Shadow Clue Four:* When we are not open to new information, new learning, or other people's views, a shadow is limiting us.
- *Shadow Clue Five:* If we react to circumstances with emotional responses disproportionate to the situation, we are right over the target of a Shadow Belief.
- *Shadow Clue Six:* When we find ourselves forcefully reacting to the limitations of others in a critical, judgmental way, we are often projecting our shadow onto others.
- *Shadow Clue Seven:* If we often experience pain, trauma, or discomfort in our body, a shadow may be attempting to rise to the surface to seek reconciliation. Listen to the wisdom of your body as you look to uncover Shadow Beliefs.

Craig, an executive I worked with, was caught in the executive syndrome of "having it all together." He feared that revealing any of his limitations would result in others perceiving him as weak or inadequate. He also honestly believed others didn't perceive his underdeveloped side. After sharing with him a 360° assessment revealing how others saw his limitations even more clearly than he did, the coaching process began. Fortunately, after he had experienced several months of coaching, a major business crisis surfaced. Here was the perfect opportunity for Craig to practice what he had learned. Clearly, he had made some mistakes leading up to the crisis. Rather than continuing the old pattern, he faced the troops, acknowledged his mistakes, and asked for their support. His co-workers were shocked and understandably hesitant at first, but they admired his courage and stepped forward to solve the crisis. Commenting on his experience, he told me, "I thought my power was in being *right*. Now I understand my power is in being *real*." Personal Mastery had begun.

> *Nothing in life is to be feared. It is only to be understood.*
>
> — Marie Curie

What happens to us when we are around people who are real and open about themselves, warts and all? We trust them. Their authenticity, vulnerability, and Personal Mastery have made them trustworthy, and we rush to their side. When asked by Charlie Rose, "What's the most important quality today for leadership?" Howard Schultz, CEO of Starbucks, replied, "To display vulnerability." In his book *Pour Your Heart into It,* Schultz says, "Although they can hire executives with many talents and skills, many CEOs discover that what they lack most is a reliable sounding board. They don't want to show vulnerability to those who report to them." He advises, "Don't be afraid to expose your vulnerabilities. Admit you don't know what you don't know. When you acknowledge your weaknesses and ask for advice, you'll be surprised how much others will help."

Vulnerability, in the words of Terry Kellogg and Marvel Harrison, is "the gift I give to those I trust, when I trust myself." A leader's authenticity is rooted and grows in a field of self-trust.

## LEADING WITH CHARACTER... LEADING BY COPING

*If leadership from the inside-out is authentic influence that creates value,* how do we go about expressing ourselves more authentically? Since the word *authenticity* comes from the same Greek root as the word *author,* I'm sure no one would be surprised that authoring your own life does not have "ten easy steps." Authenticity requires a lifelong commitment to self-discovery and self-observation.

> *Character is like a tree and reputation its shadow. The shadow is what we think of it; the tree is the real thing.*
>
> — Abraham Lincoln

However, in coaching leaders to develop more authentic dimensions of self, we have found some helpful practices to bring out the essence of who we are. When a leader approaches the question, "How authentic am I?" it is often helpful to ask some other questions first: "Where is my leadership coming from? Where are my beliefs and values coming from?" We need to consider constantly the origin of our leadership in various circumstances. Do our actions originate from deep within ourselves, or are they coming from a more superficial, limited place? Is our leadership serving only ourselves, our career and success, or is it also focused on our team and organization? Is our leadership arising from our *Character*, the essence of who we are? Or, is it derived from a pattern of *Coping*, where we tend to react to circumstances to elicit an immediate result?

Some approaches to leadership are reactive, consume energy, and produce unsustainable or undesirable results. Other approaches are transformative, add energy to the undertaking, and create value for the short and long term. The latter approaches derive from qualities of Character.

Character is the essence or core of the leader. Character is deeper and broader than any action or achievement; it springs from the essential nature of the person. Reflecting on this principle, Ralph Waldo Emerson wrote, "This is what we call character, a reserved force which acts directly as presence, and without means."

Character works to transform and open up possibilities and potential. When we are leading from our character, we exude qualities of authenticity, purpose, openness, trust, courage, congruence, and compassion. We have the ability to transform circumstances, open up possibilities, and create lasting value for ourselves and for others.

Coping protects us and helps us get through challenging circumstances. In this sense, it has value, and if used sparingly and appropriately, will serve our needs. Coping works like a muscle. We need to use it at times, but if we overuse it, the muscle will collapse. Qualities of Coping include concern for image, safety, security, comfort, or control. The Coping leader may get results but also exhibit defensiveness, fear, withdrawal, or a desire to win at all costs. He or she may exclude certain people or information.

Both approaches to leadership—leading with Character and leading by Coping—can get results. It is important to note that Coping is not in itself bad and may be needed in certain situations. For leadership, however, Character is a much better master, and Coping is a much better servant. For example, image may be a component of leadership, which can create influence and value when it is aligned with messages delivered from the leader's deeper values. On the other hand, image may be used to manipulate messages in an attempt to compensate for a leader's insecurity, and this may lead to devastating results.

Both Character and Coping are present in most leadership situations. However, we need to ask ourselves, *"Which one is my master and which one is my servant?"* When we make Character the master of our leadership and Coping the servant, we move toward better relationships and last-ing value creation.

## QUALITIES OF CHARACTER AND COPING

As leaders it is essential to learn how to build our awareness of when we are being guided by Character and when we are being guided by Coping. The following information illustrates some of the behaviors that indicate whether we are in a Character pattern or in a Coping pattern.

| CHARACTER TRANSFORMS | COPING REACTS |
|---|---|
| Opens up Possibilities and Multiplies Energy | Deals with Circumstances and Spends Energy |
| GUIDED BY: | GUIDED BY: |
| Authenticity | Image/Recognition |
| Purpose | Safety/Security/Comfort |
| Openness | Control |
| Trust | Fear |
| Balanced Concern for Self and Others | Concern for Self |
| Courage | Avoidance |
| Inclusion | Exclusion |
| Win-Win | Win-Lose |
| Balance/Centeredness | Anger |
| Agility/Resilience | Resistance to Change |
| Peaceful Presence | Uneasy Presence |
| Leader Is Bigger Than Circumstance | Circumstance Is Bigger Than the Leader |

Let's explore three examples:

*1. Image vs. Authenticity:* When we care a bit too much how we look to others and we fo-cus on getting their approval, acknowledgement, or acceptance, our leadership may be guided by an Image Coping pattern. We are in this image persona: when we try too hard to "look great"; when we present ourselves as more than we are; when we misrepresent values, beliefs, or other information to win acceptance. Recently, I was coaching the CEO of a firm and one of his key executives. Although the CEO needed to work on a few crucial growth areas, authenticity was not one of them. The key executive in his organization, however unknowingly, was caught up in her image. At a critical point in one of their interactions as the key executive was overanalyzing all the political implications of an important decision, the CEO calmly and compassionately asked, "Michelle, do you want to look good, or do you want to make a difference?" Michelle fell silent. Of course she wanted to make a difference. She needed someone to shock her out of investing herself totally in Coping and into shifting her awareness to leading from Character. In *The Corporate Mystic*, Gay Hendricks and Kate Ludeman reinforce this practice: "It is as important to challenge people about their personas as it is to love and cherish their true essence. In the business world it is dangerous to ignore people's personas. Genuinely caring for people means seeing them as they are, not blithely overlooking fatal flaws."

*2. Safety, Security, and Comfort vs. Purpose:* If our actions are principally guided by safety, security, and comfort, we are in a Coping pattern. This is a big one for most of us. It is also subtle. We are usually unaware of how staying safe is actually limiting us from new experiences and possibilities. How often have most of us thought, "When I build up enough assets, then I'll go do what I *really* want to do?" This is the voice of Coping. In the executive ranks this can be a major issue. As senior executives seek to become more comfortable financially and otherwise, do they continue to risk innovative, meaningful, out-of-the-box initiatives? Often they do not. Or, worse yet, do we postpone our real purpose and contribution for that magical future moment when we will be safe and secure enough to fully express ourselves?

I was working with a senior marketing executive who was caught in this Coping pattern. The first day I met Jack he told me he had lost his passion for his work and was preparing to leave his organization to seek a new career. After spending some time together, he shared his career-life vision: to accumulate assets in order to replace his current income and in five years start his own business. On the surface it sounded all right. As we went deeper, however, it became apparent that he had sacrificed his purpose on the altar of security and comfort. Driven by his need to accumulate money in an attempt to build his inner sense of security, he had gradually lost touch with what really gave him meaning: using his creativity and insight to help others achieve their potential. Once Jack reconnected to his purpose, he returned to his work with renewed passion and perspective.

*Character also means putting the greater good of the organization and society ahead of self-interest. It's about worrying about "what is right" rather than "who is right."*

— Noel Tichy and
Warren Bennis

When we are caught up in Coping, we seek solutions outside ourselves like changing a job, changing a career, accumulating enough money to feel secure, or changing a relationship. Too often we seek solutions in "Whats" instead of "Hows." Jack needed to re-learn *how* to show up in his life in a renewed way. He learned how to be clear about his purpose and to lead with his Character.

**3. Control vs. Openness:** If our energies are absorbed in having our world conform to our will with a desire to avoid nearly all surprise, then we are leading from a place of Coping. This is particularly challenging if we are moving from managerial to leadership roles in an organization. Managers control by virtue of their *doing*. Leaders lead by virtue of their *being*. When we are rapidly alternating between management and leadership, as is often the case, the relationship between control and openness is a constant dynamic.

Tracy, a senior-level executive for an international service firm, was clearly operating in a Control Coping pattern. It was actually her "winning formula." She viewed herself as an exceptionally competent person, and by all external measures she was. Based on a series of outstanding achievements in sales and marketing, she had been on the fast track in her company. She was known for always exceeding the need. If the organization wanted something done exceptionally well, Tracy was the one recruited for the job. Some would say she had mastered her profession—maybe even mastered some aspects of her external environment. But her external success was not based on internal mastery. Her obsessive need to control everything around her had created strain in all her relationships. Her marriage wasn't surviving her need to control. Her children were growing distant. Her friendships were suffering. The more Tracy's life started to spin out of control, the more she tried to assert control. Without understanding why, she gradually drove away nearly everyone around her. For many years, her external competence had been sufficient to help Tracy to face her life and career demands. However, her new life and leadership demands involved competence of a different order.

Tracy was a great example of the managers identified in the Brousseau, Hourihan, et al. research study cited earlier in this chapter. Tracy was a leader whose take-charge, task-focused style worked well up to a point in her career. Unwilling to pause for awareness and growth, she could easily have become among those executives whose careers hit the wall and got stuck, falling short of their potential.

Before Tracy could move to the next stage of her leadership and life effectiveness, she needed to access a platform of internal competence and character. It took a few months of coaching. She was resistant and closed at first, but slowly she came to the realization *that her excessive need to control* was based on a Shadow Belief. She had come to believe that just being herself and trusting that things would work out was not an option for her. At a crucial point in our coaching she said, "If I stopped controlling everything, my life would fall apart!" The instant she said it, the paradox hit her with full force. Her life was falling apart because she was so controlling. Yet, she felt that control was her only savior. Over time, she gained the Personal Mastery to begin trusting and to be more open to change. As her self-trust and openness grew, Tracy's ability to trust and to appreciate others grew as well. She had begun leading with Character.

# REFLECTION

## CHARACTER AND COPING

Take some time to review the rest of the qualities that guide Character and Coping listed on pages 46–49. Now, think about the qualities of Coping as you consider these questions:

- Which of these qualities are most prevalent for you?

- What is going on in those times?

- How do you feel?

- What fears, limitations, or inadequacies do you avoid when you are in a Coping pattern?

- How can you challenge yourself to move out of Coping and into Character more often?

Now, reflect on the qualities of Character, and consider these questions.

- Which of these qualities are more prevalent for you?

- What is going on in those times?

- How do you feel?

- What fears do you have to face to lead from Character?

- How can you continue to lead from Character in more situations in the future?

As we have seen, Character transforms whereas Coping tends to be more of a reactive, survival mode. When we are in a Coping pattern, we tend to see the problems of life as existing outside ourselves. We say to ourselves, "If I could only change this person or that situation, then everything would be fine." But life's problems are rarely resolved by only changing the external situation. Lasting solutions involve dealing with our internal situation in order to transform the external circumstance. To illustrate this principle, imagine Nelson Mandela several years ago saying, "I think I need to leave South Africa. The situation here is just too big a problem. These people just don't get it. I need to go to a more comfortable, accommodating country." It sounds humorous even to imagine this scenario with a person of so much Character. When Character and purpose are weak, then our initial Coping response is usually to leave or escape our situation. When purpose is strong, leaders transform many of the circumstances they encounter. Obviously, there may be times when we need to leave or walk away from a situation for self-preservation. However, if our first response is consistently to exit challenging circumstances, then we probably need to work on leaning into Character more often.

It's important to note that Personal Mastery is not about eliminating Coping. It is about increasing Character to such a degree that Character is primary and Coping is secondary. Coping exists for a reason—to protect us and to deal with stressful situations—so, we really don't want to eliminate it completely. It serves a purpose. We do want to favor Character so that this more substantial way to lead becomes the master of our behavior more often. To have Character supporting Coping—the inner supporting the outer—is the goal of Personal Mastery.

Leading with Character is not easy. The CEO of a rapidly growing firm shared this comment with me: "I hate to admit it, but most organizations reward Coping. We talk about Character, but we reward Coping. We extol the values of trust, inclusion, and adding value, but we consistently reward control and image. Most of us are unwilling to do the hard work and to take the personal risk to lead from Character."

Unfortunately, executive coaching programs often reinforce refining Coping rather than fostering Character. Executives are coached *how to act* instead of *how to be*. It's a charm-school process that produces only superficial, short-term results. Executives are "coached" to polish the exterior, but rarely does any real substantial and sustained growth take place. Under sufficient stress, all the old patterns return.

> *Corporate Mystics develop a kind of double vision, at once able to see the mask and the essential person inside. . . . They know that we all have personas that are wrapped around our true essence, but they also know that we are not our personas.*
> — Gay Hendricks and Kate Ludeman

To be effective, executive coaching needs to build awareness of the limiting aspects of Coping behaviors so that Character can be primary and Coping secondary. Penetrating Coping mechanisms to allow Character to come forth requires sophisticated coaching that deals with the whole person.

## UNDERSTANDING OUR OWNER'S MANUAL

Many of us know more about our favorite vacation spot, sports team, or running shoes than we do about ourselves. In order to break out of old patterns and grow as a whole person, we need to answer the "Who am I?" question. As we take on this question, we may get snickers from our own internal critic. Or, we may return with a quick answer that superficially reflects the roles we play vs. who we really are.

The other day I sat down with a CEO for an initial coaching session. With a bit of nervous bravado the executive proclaimed, "Kevin, you know, I know myself pretty well." Honestly,

> *The wisest mind has something yet to learn.*
> — George Santayana

I've been in situations like this so many times I envisioned a subtitle across his chest that read, "He doesn't *know* himself very well at all." On the other hand, when I meet with someone who admits, "You know, I understand some aspects of myself, but others are still a mystery to me," then my envisioned subtext says, "This person *knows* himself pretty well."

Perhaps the reason most people think they know themselves well is that their experience of their inner world is restricted to very narrow boundaries. Few people would admit that they know everything *outside* themselves. We all understand how unfathomable external knowledge and information is. We see the external world as huge. Our inner life, however, is defined too often in a very restricted way. When we get on the path to Personal Mastery, we begin to glimpse how deep, broad, and unbounded our inner life really is. When people casually say, "I know myself," all too often they are really saying, "I know my limited state of self-knowledge." There are no limits within us. There is no end to Personal Mastery. It is bigger, deeper, and grander than the external world we think is so vast. Begin your journey by considering life's big questions: "Who are you? Where are you headed? Why are you going there?" That darn soldier just crossed our path again, didn't he?

Personal Mastery is about comprehending the vehicle, our character, that brings us to our destination. There's just one problem: We've temporarily lost the "owner's manual." It's like buying a high performance sports car without learning how to drive it. Sure we know how to drive, but we just don't understand how to drive *that* vehicle. How are we ever going to arrive safely at our desired destination when we don't understand that taking a curve at 65 miles an hour on a wet road at midnight with a certain suspension system is an invitation for disaster? That's exactly how many leaders lead—barreling down the freeway of life without any real mastery of their owner's manual. So how can we start to understand our owner's manual? How can we begin to uncover our identity and maneuver this "vehicle"? The following reflection will help you get on the path. But remember, no one else can give you this insight. You must give it to yourself. This is the beginning of the process.

# REFLECTION

## CLARIFYING OUR STRENGTHS AND GROWTH AREAS

Take your time. Be thoughtful. The questions are designed to be thought-provoking, so don't rush through them. Read all the questions first, and begin the exercise by answering the ones that come easiest. Use a notepad to sketch out longer responses.

1. Imagine yourself observing a dear friend talking about you with heartfelt love and admiration. What would your friend be saying?

2. When you are energized and inspired, what particular personality traits or strengths are being expressed by you?

3. What are some of your Conscious Beliefs about yourself?

4. What are you most afraid of?

5. When you are leading with Character, what qualities come forth? Do certain situations inhibit or express your character more?

6. When you are leading by Coping, what qualities come forth? What beliefs or fears are generating these states of mind or emotion?

7. When during your life have you felt most completely yourself—not meeting others' expectations, but just being centered in expressing who you are?

8. What steps can you take in your life to create more times like this?

9. What do other people consistently tell you that you need to work on or develop? What new behavior are you committed to practicing?

10. What is your unique value proposition as a leader? If you were a brand, what brand of leadership would you be?

11. What do you hope people will thank you for contributing at the end of your life?

12. If you witnessed your funeral, what do you hope the eulogy would say?

As we will continue to explore throughout this book, Personal Mastery is not a recent phenomenon; it is imbedded in the nature of the human experience. Nearly all significant systems of human development through the ages have valued it. More contemporary thinkers like Warren Bennis, Stephen Covey, Daniel Goleman, Peter Senge, Richard Leider, and so many others have recognized its value-creating influence. Many human development systems like client-centered therapy, cognitive behavioral coaching, rational-emotive therapy, adult learning theory, transformative learning, NLP, Landmark Forum, humanistic coaching, and psychodynamic coaching certainly align with what we have been discussing. Many of these methodologies could be helpful on your journey to Personal Mastery. An excellent article by John Passmore in *Consulting Psychology Journal: Practice and Research*, March 2007, connects many of these approaches to coaching and development.

## EIGHT POINTS FOR PERSONAL MASTERY

Keep in mind the following principles as you begin to master your ability to lead with more awareness and authenticity.

*1. Take Total Responsibility:* Commit yourself to the path of Personal Mastery. Only you can commit to it, and only you can walk your own path to it. No one else can motivate you. No one else can do it for you. A mentor cannot do it for you. Your organization or clients cannot do it for you. As Hermann Hesse wrote in *Demian*, "Each man had only one genuine vocation—to find the way to himself." Personal Mastery is the one life experience we must give ourselves. No one else is "in the loop." Walt Whitman wrote, "Not I—not anyone else—can travel that road for you; you must learn to travel it for yourself."

No matter what life or leadership challenges we face, no matter what circumstances we encounter; we are responsible. As we advance, we notice that we are more self-validated, self-recognized, self-trusting. As we increasingly assume responsibility for the life we are creating, we are prepared to assume responsibility for leading others. The foundation of genuine leadership is built with self-leadership, self-responsibility, and self-trust.

*2. Bring Beliefs to Conscious Awareness:* Commit to the process of clarifying your Conscious Beliefs and your Shadow Beliefs. Practice by pausing to reflect on how some of these beliefs open you up and how others close you down. Practice reinforcing the ones that open up possibilities and energize you, as well as others. Reconsider the ones that limit possibilities and drain energy. Remind yourself of the Personal Mastery mantra: "As you believe, so shall you lead."

> *The leader for today and the future will be focused on how to be—how to develop quality, character, mind-set, values, principles, and courage.*
>
> — Frances Hesselbein

**3. Develop Awareness of Character and Coping:** Develop an awareness of when you are leading with the qualities of Character and when you are being led by the qualities of Coping. Instead of overinvesting in Coping, commit your energies to leading with Character. Doing so requires that you courageously examine the beliefs, fears, and limitations generating the qualities of Coping. Facing these limiting filters will free up energy to experience new learning from the outside, as well as to express new potentiality from within. Transform your approach to leading by making Character the master and Coping the servant.

**4. Practice Personal Mastery with Others:** Practicing Personal Mastery requires risk and vulnerability. It means placing ourselves in situations where we may not be accepted or validated by others for who we are or what we think or believe. If we do not take this risk, we too often will be led by the expectations of others. As a result, we might unknowingly compromise our integrity. As you practice Personal Mastery with others, keep these thoughts in mind:

> *Leadership and learning are indispensable to each other.*
>
> —John F. Kennedy

- Listen to your authentic inner voice for what you really think and feel vs. what others want you to think and feel.
- Be mindful when "creating" others in your image.
- Be mindful when "being created" by others in their image.
- Practice the strength of vulnerability; notice how it opens up relationships and teams.
- Be aware when you are wasting too much time and energy judging others and trying to change them.
- Be there for people when they need you. Be there not only for the purpose of giving advice or being appreciated for your support but also just to give the gift of your presence.
- Practice sharing your genuine thoughts, feelings, joys, successes, concerns, and fears with people. Let your openness be the catalyst to open up the culture around you.

**5. Listen to Feedback:** Even though Personal Mastery is self-validating, sometimes other people hold keys to our self-knowledge. As Edith Wharton wrote, "There are two ways of spreading light; to be the candle or the mirror that reflects it." How often have we resisted the input of others only to realize later that their comments were right on target? Is it possible their insights were greater than we were prepared to assimilate at the time? Rather than spending our energy defending a rigid state of self-awareness, we can think of Personal Mastery as a continuous, lifelong, learning process. Life experiences are opportunities to learn and to develop. Colleagues are there to coach and mentor. Consider all input from others as potentially instructive. Those around us may be holding the torches to light our path to Personal Mastery. Personal Mastery involves the delicate paradox of being open to learning from others without allowing ourselves to be unduly created by them.

*6. Consider Finding a Coach:* There is nothing "wrong" with getting support. In fact, recent studies have shown that companies now use coaching 75 percent of the time to optimize performance vs. "fixing" problems. Having a coach as your partner during your growth process might be the most "right" thing you ever do. You might be pleasantly surprised to know how much an objective, experienced coach can accelerate your personal and leadership progress. Coaching can free self-awareness and facilitate some helpful directions for growth. Be sure to take some time to find the best coach for you. Initially, experience personal sessions with a few people. Share your story. Then, gauge your chemistry and values connections with each potential coach, as well as his or her experience level with your type of situation. Quality professional support can offer a significant growth experience; is a time to be yourself and to get clarity. It is an opportunity to explore new ways to live and to lead.

*7. Avoid Confusing Self-Delusion with Self-Awareness:* In a survey of business executives published in *Business Week*, August 2007, executives were asked, "Are you in the top 10 percent of leadership performance?" Their responses: 90 percent said yes. Hmmm. Someone has to be wrong here! Self-assessment can be the least accurate leadership assessment. To remedy this, use grounded, validated assessments with a solid research history to ensure that your growing self-awareness is real. Using instruments like *Decision Styles*, *Voices®*, *Choices®*, *Hogan®*, *Myers Briggs Type Indicator®*, *California Psychological Inventory® (CPI 260)*, and *Zenger/Folkman®*, among others, can accelerate your accurate self-awareness. Auditing your self-assessments against these research-based assessments can challenge your personal growth to new levels. However, be aware that no one tool can capture your entire profile. Assessment instruments can be very helpful only as part of your overall personal mastery growth process. Be sure to have at least one tool that is inside-out (personality, values, or preferences assessments) and one that is outside-in (i.e., 360° assessment).

*8. Be Agile:* Sometimes the strengths that helped you lead in your present state of development may hamper your future chances of success. You may recall the news photos of Karl

Wallenda's final high-wire performance as he attempted to cross between two tall buildings. As he made his way on the wire, using his famous balancing pole, an intense wind came up. Everyone watching immediately understood Wallenda's dilemma. As the wind blew him off the wire, he clutched onto his balancing pole. All he needed to do was to let go of the pole and grab the wire. But because the pole had saved his balance so many times before, he held onto it even as he fell to the ground. He held onto what he knew best even when it no longer served him. Understand and appreciate your strengths, but also be flexible and adaptable. Many strong winds may be coming your way.

# LEADERSHIP GROWTH PLAN
## PERSONAL MASTERY

It's time to step back. Shift out of "I'm reading a book" mode. Instead of treating this book as an interesting intellectual exercise, sit back and capture some insights and commitments that can make a genuine difference in your life and in your leadership. Pause to identify some areas to build Awareness, Commitment, and Practice. (For more on building Awareness, Commitment, and Practice, see Action Mastery.) Aim high. Also, note potential obstacles and success measures. As you do this, keep asking yourself, "What will really make a difference to enhance my authenticity and awareness?"

1. Areas for Building Awareness:

- _____
- _____
- _____

2. New Commitments to Make:

- _____
- _____
- _____

3. New Practices to Begin:

- _____
- _____
- _____

4. Potential Obstacles:

- _____
- _____
- _____

5. Timeline and Measures of Success:

- _____
- _____
- _____

# LEADERSHIP GROWTH PLAN
## PERSONAL MASTERY EXAMPLE

1. Areas to Build Awareness: Image and control are more prevalent than I thought; need to build awareness of my self-limiting belief regarding "never achieving/doing enough."

2. New Commitments to Make:

   A. Move from control to trust to let others participate more.
   B. Let go of some of my image needs.
   C. Explore my need to do so much.

3. New Practices to Begin:

   A. Do 360° feedback.
   B. Find a coach.
   C. Get colleague and spouse participation/feedback.

4. Potential Obstacles:

   A. Fear of change.
   B. Fear of failure if I change things too much.
   C. Will colleagues and the organization accept changes?

5. Timeline and Measures of Success:

   A. In three months, have people acknowledge that I am less controlling and more trusting.
   B. In six months, have several people notice that I am dropping my image and being more authentic.
   C. In one month, get home before 6:30 P.M., four nights a week.

# CHAPTER TWO

# PURPOSE MASTERY

## *Leading on Purpose*

Core Purpose is the high performance intersection where our talents and our values come together. It is the value-creating, catalytic moment when our gifts make a difference. When we split off our values from our talents, or vice versa, we compromise purpose . . . and enduring performance.

About a year ago, Benton came to us for coaching. While he was highly valued by his company for his results and intellect, he was so entrenched in non-listening and aggressive behavior I thought coaching would be hopeless. I honestly didn't think it would be worthwhile to invest the resources to coach him. At first it was a struggle, but eventually Benton surprised us and genuinely engaged in the process. We helped him to see that his Core Talents—his intellect, drive for results, ability to get things done—were coming through consistently at work. However, at times his Core Values—compassion and connection—were not. Interestingly, when working with his own team, Benton's Core Talents and Core Values were present and operating in sync. The same was true at home. Benton was a popular coach of his daughter's soccer teams. He was present and involved with his wife and other members of his family. But when interacting with his peers and higher-level leaders, Benton introverted his Core Values. He split them off from his Core Talents. In these situations, he was competitive, closed, and defensive. His talents became liabilities. A big shadow was cast because his values were hidden with certain groups. Benton surprised us. Once he realized what he was doing, he found the awareness and new behaviors energizing. He wanted to change. His HR person called us and said, "This is incredible. Never in my career have we seen such a remarkable transformation." Now, the feedback from Benton's peers and higher-level managers is that he is listening, and he is improving significantly in building trust. Occasionally, he will slip. But more often than not, he catches himself and steps forward with both his talents and values. Once Benton got the whole picture, saw the consequences of splitting off his values from his talents, he was committed to working toward being in that sweet spot, Core Purpose, more often.

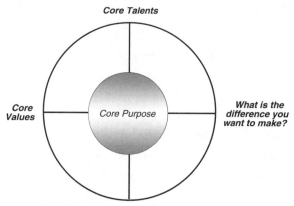

## DISCOVERING THE SWEET SPOT

While Core Values provide an understanding of what we are motivated to pursue and what we want to influence, Core Talents tell us what gifts we have and how we can have an im-

> *The secret of success is constancy of purpose.*
> — Benjamin Disraeli

pact. In career, life, and leadership situations that are fulfilling, our Core Talents and Values will tend to complement each other. Richard Leider, Eldership coach and author of *The Power of Purpose: Creating Meaning in Your Life and Work*, says that Purpose is strengthened when we "align the WHO behind the WHAT." Therefore, identifying our Core Talents is the first step in doing just that. When we identify our Core Talents and our Core Values, we begin to articulate our Core Purpose—that sweet spot where we align our talents to satisfy our values, thus optimizing both our gifts and our contributions.

Knowing our particular combination of talents and values allows us to apply them consciously in a more powerful, tangible manner.

## IDENTIFYING CORE TALENTS

All of us have particular skills or domains of life in which we excel. Some come to us almost naturally; others evolve through study and hard work. Regardless of their origin and path of development, Core Talents are those that make us feel energized or in "flow," as scientist Mihaly Csikszentmihalyi would call it. Csikszentmihalyi, well known for his research and writings on "flow" or "optimal experience," explains that among other things, when in "flow" we lose self-consciousness. We may lose track of time, not even realizing how long and hard we are working. The experience is so enjoyable, we would do it even if we didn't have to. At the end of a day although we may be tired, we don't feel drained. Instead, we feel a strong, inner sense of fulfillment, and we look forward to the next day with eager anticipation. Dr. Martin E. P. Seligman, in his work on "learned optimism," calls Core Talents "signature strengths." He says that when we use our "signature strengths" in work, we increase our opportunities for more happiness in our lives. When we turn our work-life into our "life's work," it is the most satisfying because it is done for its own sake and for the people it serves rather than for only an extrinsic reward.

# REFLECTION

## CORE TALENTS

Think back over your career and your life. Recall those times when you felt most energized in applying your talents to the task at hand. You might have been engaged in something more personal or seemingly inconsequential, such as coaching a golf partner or writing to a friend. Or, you might have been involved in something bigger, more visible or dramatic, such as envisioning a large presentation or planning a company strategy. Think about those times when you felt you were at your best, you were most energized and engaged. Jot down some of those instances on a piece of paper, in a notebook, or in a journal. Ask yourself and respond to the following questions and statements:

1. What gifts can people count on me for?

2. When I am making a difference/creating value, my talents that "show up" are:

3. Other people consistently tell me I make a difference by:

4. When I am working with others, and we are most energized and engaged, I am contributing:

5. I just can't help contributing:

6. In summary, my Core Talents—the gifts that I have that make a difference—are:

## RECOGNIZING CORE VALUES

A true leadership guru, Warren Bennis contends that the purpose of leadership is to "remind people what is important." Reminding others what is important certainly penetrates the essence of leadership, doesn't it? However, before we can remind others what is important, we first need to know what is important. Sounds easy? Often, it is not. We all like to think we know where we stand and what we value, but knowing our authentic values—the standards and guiding principles rooted deep in our hearts and guts—is one of the most challenging aspects of self-discovery. Although many individuals prefer to take the easier route and avoid it, the work of identifying real values is worth the effort on many fronts. In *Purpose: The Starting Point of Great Companies*, Nikos Mourkogiannis cites a survey of leading corporate executives, conducted in 2004 by the Aspen Institute and Booz Allen Hamilton. This survery confirmed a connection between financial performance and values, "showing that financial leaders were more likely to make 'values' explicit by codifying or articulating them."

When we asked one client what was important to him, he responded by rattling off the typical list: family, working hard, making a difference, serving others. Like our client, many of us would automatically recite: "My family is the most important thing in my life. Contributing to the welfare of the less fortunate is crucial. Mentoring my employees is a high priority." Well, they all sound good, and they are all values worthy of high regard. But *are they really your most important values*? Or, have you blindly adopted them from your environment? Although we would be reluctant to admit it, our spoken values are often a reflection of what our family believes, what our organization says is important, what the latest business book says. However, *our authentic values and sense of meaning* are deeper than this. Authentic values are forged in the traumas and privileges of our unique life story.

While coaching Michael, a highly effective leader, I learned that on the surface he was a great communicator. He was articulate, direct, and clear. If anything, he was a bit too polished. To his surprise, he received feedback that people didn't trust him. This information came from not just a couple of people but several key colleagues and staff members, people crucial to his success. The news was a complete shock to him. Reeling from the feedback, he said, "I work hard on my communication skills and tell it like it is. My intentions are good. What's wrong?"

To help Michael discover the answer, we began examining how people perceived him, and how he perceived himself. Eventually, it was clear. Under stress or crisis, Michael didn't

*The highest courage is to dare to appear to be what one is.*

— John Lancaster Spalding

inspire and move people. The more a crisis heated up, the more polished and detached his communication became. People couldn't connect with him. They couldn't sense where he was coming from, what he considered important and compelling. As a result, people didn't trust him. They felt he was smooth, slick, and calm, but he wasn't real. He wasn't drawing from anything truly meaningful from within his life story.

Michael realized that he couldn't be a more authentic and inspiring leader by further refining his presentation skills; he had to look deeply and honestly at what was important to him. After some intensive work unearthing his most relevant and profound career and life learning experiences, he began to connect to his deeper values. He started sharing true stories—

*If you do not express your own original ideas, if you do not listen to your own being, you will have betrayed yourself.*

— Rollo May

*the language of leadership*—to emphasize his message. Under crisis, he shared a story about his first career failure and what he had learned about overcoming obstacles. While relating his father's sage advice about running the family business, he unexpectedly choked up in the middle of the anecdote. He began to show up as a whole person, and people responded. Slowly but surely, Michael rebuilt trust brick by brick, value by value, and story by story.

# REFLECTION

## CORE VALUES

Remind yourself of what is important to you based on the lessons your life experiences have taught you. These questions and statements will help you consider what you stand for as a leader, what your real values are. Reflect on them, and write your responses on a piece of paper, in a notebook, or in a journal.

1. What has your life taught you about what is precious and valuable?

2. What have the traumas and losses in your life taught you about what is most important?

3. What have the privileges of your life taught you about what is of value?

4. What is worth risking your life for?

5. _____ gives me the greatest meaning in life or work.

6. In summary, my Core Values—what I value and stand for as a person/leader—are:

## REVEALING CORE PURPOSE

Remember Michael? We also helped him to uncover his Core Purpose—how his gifts serve the needs of others. At first this was a foreign idea. "I just do my job and get results!" he insisted. "But how do you bring your whole self into doing your job and getting results?" I pressed. "What is your unique, meaningful contribution?" After having him chart Five Fantasy Lives he would most like to live, we debriefed the common characteristic of these lives and clarified his Core Purpose: *Applying insight and vision to realize new possibilities*. When he made his Core Purpose conscious, his realization was stunning. We could feel it in the room—a deep, reverent clarity about who he really was. With this heightened awareness,

> *I slept and dreamt that*
> *life was joy,*
> *I awoke and saw that*
> *life was service,*
> *I acted and behold,*
> *service was joy.*
>
> — Tagore

we then looked at each part of his life—family, career, community involvement, himself—and analyzed how aligned or misaligned his Core Purpose was with each of these.

To Michael's surprise, his Core Purpose had the lowest alignment or application to himself. So the real work was to strengthen his own connection to his Core Purpose so that he could bring forward more of his "I," his power-of-voice, into his leadership. How could he be even more courageous in realizing more possibilities? How could he be more insightful and visionary in developing himself? How could he realize new possibilities in the ways he showed up in his own life? As he did this personal alignment work, a foundation was built to bring his Core Purpose into all facets of his life. Later he commented in a coaching session, "Core Purpose is like my compass. It helps to point all my energy, behaviors, and decisions in the right direction."

Core Purpose is the "true north," as Bill George tells us, that keeps our career and life decisions in harmony with our authentic talents, values, and meaningful contribution. When considering purpose in our lives, we often confuse the "what" with the "how." We ask ourselves, "What am I going to be when I grow up?" The answer we're looking for is a job description—doctor, lawyer, business owner—not a state of being—wise, energetic, compassionate, at peace. Later, we wonder what we'll do with ourselves when we retire. Always focusing on the external manifestation, we may miss the foundation of purpose. To find that foundation, we need to ask, "How am I going to make a difference now . . . when I 'grow up' . . . and when I retire?"

A short while ago I learned a valuable lesson on this dynamic in an unexpected setting. In our building, our offices and restrooms were cleaned daily by a young woman, recently arrived from Africa, who was always gloriously dressed in the colorful garb of her native country. I was always struck by the delight with which she approached her seemingly mundane duties. One evening she was joyously singing a beautiful song as she worked away. Approaching her in the hallway, I commented, "You really love your work, don't you?" Her demeanor stiffened, and she became very serious. She set down her mop, looked piercingly into me, and with a penetrating, instructive tone said, "Sir, I *do not love* to clean bathrooms." Then with a soft, warm heart she said, "I *love while* I clean bathrooms!"

I felt blessed to be mentored by such a wise woman, and her advice reminded me of a wonderful story. There once was a leader of a major monastery in China who was known for his purposeful teaching. However, instead of lecturing people on his teachings and getting lost in theory and concept, he would demonstrate his purposefulness by sweeping the steps of the monastery with all his being. People would come to the entry inquiring about the leader of the monastery, and the "sweeper" would say, "The teacher is teaching now." Since most of the aspirants were focused on looking for something external, "the teacher," they rarely recognized that the entire teaching and meaning were present in how the sweeper approached his work-life.

Purpose is present in *how we show up* in whatever activity we engage. Jimmy Carter's book, *Beyond the White House: Waging Peace, Fighting Disease, Building Hope*, opens with a wonderful story about this. During an interview, Barbara Walters asked the former president to identify the time in his life that was "best." After taking a moment to think, President Carter replied, "By far, my best years are those I'm enjoying now, since Rosalynn and I left the White House." I was struck by how purposeful a person would have to be to not think that being president was the highlight of his or her career and contribution. How many of us are pursuing title and recognition at the expense of purpose? Jimmy and Rosalynn Carter are exceptional examples of ordinary people, who live their lives every day authentically and deeply connected to their purpose regardless of title, position, or recognition. They lead from who they are; they lead from their Core Purpose. As a leader, how are you showing up? Are you lecturing others about how things should be, or are you purposefully leading by example? Is only part of your being in your work, or are you fully present in how you lead?

Purpose is not a goal to be set. It is not something we create. It is not some "great idea" we come up with. It is something we discover. Purpose is there all the time, and it's waiting for us. It's our duty, our role in life; it's what we have been prepared to express. In *Synchronicity—The Inner Path of Leadership*, Joseph Jaworski writes, "It is the call to service, giving our life over to something larger than ourselves, the call to become what we were meant to become—the call to achieve our vital design." If we ignore this calling, no amount of external success can make us feel complete.

The implications of discovering purpose go far beyond our profession or career. They impact all of our life. A client of ours discovered that her life's purpose was "to use her influencing and counseling gift to be of service to people." While this purpose could potentially

*Ever more, people today have the means to live, but not the meaning to live for.*
— Victor Frankl

influence all sorts of career outcomes in teaching, consulting, professional associations, nonprofit groups, or business in general, it also would impact her personal, spiritual, and community life. Purpose is the broad context that integrates all our life experiences. It is the *defining thread* that runs through and connects life's divergent experiences.

Jack Hawley writes in *Reawakening the Spirit in Work*, "Our life direction is about moving into the vacant upstairs flat." Purpose is that home within, that place where our talents, values, and spirit reside. It's there all the time, waiting for our arrival. We may have been too busy "living our life downstairs" to even notice.

## "MOVING UPSTAIRS" TO OUR PURPOSE

A few years ago, I worked with a client who recently realized that she had been "living downstairs." She entered my office in a down mood and after very little chitchat blurted out, "Cake mixes don't give any meaning to my life!" Caught off guard, I started laughing. She wasn't amused and said, "I'm serious; I used to love my job, but it just doesn't seem important to me anymore." After I worked with her for a while, she began to explore the contents of her "upstairs flat." Her discovery centered around "using her innovative and conceptual gifts to enrich and to nourish people's lives." She had been "living downstairs" for so long that she actually thought that cake mixes were supposed to give meaning to her life! Her purpose became overshadowed by her day-to-day focus. When she finally uncovered her purpose—to enrich and to nourish others through innovation—her attitude about her job changed, her creativity returned, and her performance soared. Her life wasn't about cake mixes; it was about being a creative force to enhance people's lives. This realization permeated her entire life situation, and nearly everyone in her life sensed her renewal.

## DIVING BENEATH THE SURFACE TO OUR PURPOSE

Unfortunately, most people tend to limit purpose by viewing it only as something external. To really understand the value of purpose we need to dive beneath the surface.

I worked once with the president of a large company based in Asia who was struggling with purpose and meaning in his life. Even though he had strong family values and other interests, he was having a difficult time comprehending his life's purpose as something bigger than his career. All his life he had aspired to achieve his current career goal. Along the way he had made many difficult personal sacrifices to achieve it. Now that he had achieved his "purpose," he was feeling, "Is this it?"

Although my client had a vague sense that there must be more than his achieved goal, he couldn't articulate what it was. At one of our sessions I asked him, "What happens when a company defines itself by its products and results instead of its underlying competencies and values?" He immediately responded, "Well, they eventually perish because, as the marketplace changes, their products become obsolete." I then said, "What happens to the company that defines itself by its Core Values and capabilities?" He again quickly responded, "They thrive because they continually adapt themselves to the changing market." Then I said, "So, which type of 'company' are you?" He immediately became aware of how his external definition was limiting him. He realized that his purpose was more than simply achieving the next career goal. His passion was deeper than that. It was about helping people to develop and to grow. His entire personal and professional life had demonstrated this passion. It was the "lens" through which he viewed his entire life. It was present in his family, his relationships, *and* his work. It was what he was really all about. He grew to understand that purpose was broader than his goals. It was the foundation on which he had built his life.

## PURPOSE IS BIGGER AND DEEPER THAN OUR GOALS

How often have you heard someone say about extraordinary people, "He was born to do this. She was born to do that." It is as if the "thing" was their only goal, their only reason for being. What happens when the "thing" is done or the career is over? Does that mean the person no longer has a purpose? Are these people then expendable from life? *Purpose is the flow of life through us as it serves all those it touches.* Sometimes we may inhibit or ignore this flow, but it is always there seeking expression. How it manifests itself depends on our ability to open up to it and the particular circumstances we may be facing at the time. Purpose is constant. The manifestation of purpose is always changing.

I once had a client who asked me, "How can I tell the difference between obsessively or compulsively driven behavior and purposefully driven behavior? It is difficult to tell them apart sometimes." Purpose releases energy. The higher the purpose, the greater the energy. Purpose also frees us. The more profound the purpose, the greater the sense of freedom. Purpose opens up possibilities. Obsession or compulsion drains our energy and binds us to the activity itself. Less joy, less energy, and less freedom are the results. When observing the passionate, focused

*Man can face any "what" if he has a big enough "why."*
— Friedrich Nietzche

behavior of people, it can sometimes be difficult to know if the observed are being passionately obsessive or passionately purposeful. If the behavior is adding energy, joy, and fulfillment to them and others, then it is probably coming from a purposeful place. In Mihaly Csikszentimihalyi's words,

Flow lifts the course of life to a different level. Alienation gives way to involvement, enjoyment replaces boredom, helplessness turns into a feeling of control, and psychic energy works to reinforce the sense of self, instead of being lost in the service of external goals. When experience is intrinsically rewarding, life is justified in the present, instead of being held hostage to a hypothetical future gain.

## CONNECTING THE INNER WITH THE OUTER: PURPOSE, AUTHENTICITY, AND CONGRUENCE

When we look at the lives of highly effective people and value creating organizations, often there is a common theme. Their reason for being is clearer to them. This connection, sense of meaning, love for what they do, often drives their success. When we are more certain of what we stand for, what is genuinely important, then it is much more difficult to keep us from achieving our objectives. Achievements come as natural by-products of our connection to purpose.

*The world of ours has been constructed like a superbly written novel; we pursue the tale with avidity, hoping to discover the plot.*
— Sir Arthur Keith

Bob Eichinger and Michael Lombardo, Co-Founders of Lominger International, tell us that "much research has shown that organizations with sound and inspiring missions and visions do better in the marketplace. Sound missions and visions motivate and guide people on how to allot their time and how to make choices." In *Good to Great*, Jim Collins writes about the preservation of what he calls "core ideology," the combination of Core Values and Core Purpose as a feature of enduring companies that went "from good to great to built to last." Collins explains that there are not necessarily any "right" or "wrong" values, but there is the necessity to have them and to hold onto them. Core Purpose, a "reason for being beyond making money," is the partner of Core Values. "Enduring great companies preserve their core values and purpose while their business strategies and operating practices endlessly adapt to a changing world."

However, if any company, especially a fast-paced, growth company, is going to be able to hold fast to its rock-solid values and purpose, its leader must be able to comprehend and articulate on a moment's notice his or her own Core Purpose. Howard Schultz, CEO of Starbucks, warns,

> Whatever your culture, your values, your guiding principles, you have to take steps to inculcate them in the organization early in its life so that they can guide every decision, every hire, every strategic objective you set. Whether you are the CEO or a lower level employee, the single most important thing you do at work each day is communicate your values to others.

## UNFOLDING THE DEFINING THREAD OF PURPOSE

You may think that I have "this purpose thing" all figured out. Actually, the only thing I know for sure is that it's an endless journey. Many years ago I was convinced about the concept of purpose, yet my own purpose was not crystal-clear to me. I began to take my own advice. Over and over I asked myself four crucial questions: "What am I passionate about? Why do I pursue the work-life I do? What are my gifts? What energizes me and others most?" Again and again, I explored these questions.

Over time, glimpses of this elusive "thing" called purpose emerged. Sometimes in a quiet moment an insight would come. Other times, while I was working, I would feel its energetic presence. Occasionally a glimpse would appear in a personal relationship. As the months passed, I began to understand it more clearly. One day I was running along one of my favorite wooded trails beside a creek. I wasn't trying to sort things out, but my "defining thread" was rolling out like a ball of yarn thrown across the floor. This "thread" seemed to connect all the significant experiences of my life: Whether I was seeking my education in psychology, teaching people how to meditate, being a career consultant, being an executive coach, writing, or speaking, it was all about one thing: *Using presence, passion, and purpose to be a catalyst for growth.* The insight was so clear it actually stopped me in my tracks. Absorbed in the power of this realization, I assimilated this "connecting thread." It was a defining moment. My purpose had always been operating, but the power of the moment was bringing it to conscious awareness. From that point forward, my life had more conscious context. Decisions no longer seemed ambiguous or reactive. I started to understand why I was doing the things I was doing and how I was expressing my talents to make a contribution. My reason for being—my reason for leading—was starting to come into focus.

A leader of purpose gives people a reason to attach themselves to something bigger than themselves; a leader without purpose may have positional power but lack authentic followers. Core Purpose is the deeply seeded impulse we all have to make a difference. When we align with our purpose, our voice is strong, our energy is optimal, our gifts are manifest, and our service is passionate.

## SIX THOUSAND DAYS

While leading a team-building session in Europe last year to help foster a more positive culture in a global company, the CEO had arranged for the group to visit a nearby Tibetan monastery. The group was a bit reluctant, but the monk was very gracious. He greeted us, seated us in the meditation hall, and immediately engaged us in a provocative conversation. Although I've been fortunate to learn from many great teachers, I was unprepared when he singled me out at the very beginning of the discourse and asked me, "How many days do you have left to live?" I was stunned by the profound question, but surprisingly the answer flashed in my mind. "Six thousand," I said. The monk replied, "That sounds about right.

*What lies behind us and what lies before us are tiny matters compared to what lies within us.*

— Oliver Wendell Holmes

So, if you have 6,000 days, do you want to waste any of them? Do you want to waste any of those days in frustration, anger, or not living your purpose?" The power, depth, and personal relevance of his existential question simultaneously disturbed me and inspired me into a reflective state of mind, where I was "forced" to wrestle with it. It reminded me how one powerful question can change our lives . . . and how precious every moment of life is.

Alex Gorsky, Company Group Chairman, Ethicon, a Johnson & Johnson business unit, shared his own poignant story about the significance of not wasting time. As a young cadet at a military academy, Alex sat in the audience with his classmates during their orientation while the Dean of Academic Affairs addressed the entire corps. He told the first-year cadets, "Some of you will succeed. Some will fail. What will make the difference is how you use your 'scraps of time.'" Pause for a moment, and think. How are you using your "scraps of time"? By reminding ourselves of the limited amount of time we really have, a positive tension arises, urging us to do something significant, something grounded in service. The monk's challenging question followed me for days and circulates within me still, just as does the dean's admonition. Both remind me not to waste a day . . . on-purpose.

Take a little time now to ask yourself the same question the wise monk asked me, "How many days do you have left to live?" Really calculate it and come up with a number. Now, ask yourself, "Knowing the limited number of days I have, what do I want to do?" What is your purpose-fueled strategy for how you are going to lead and live those days?

Core Purpose frames all our life and career experiences into a meaningful whole. When we understand purpose, all the challenging experiences of our lives serve to forge identity, character, and meaning. Although life may be challenging, every experience becomes our teacher, and every challenge an opportunity through which we learn and live more purposefully. When we lack purpose, immediate circumstances dominate our awareness and overshadow our reason for being. Life tends to lose connection with its true nature. Teilhard de Chardin wrote, "We are not human beings having a spiritual experience. We are spiritual beings having a human experience." Purpose is spirit seeking expression; awareness of it allows us to see our lives more clearly from the inside-out.

You may be thinking that all this seems a bit abstract and esoteric. However, Core Purpose may be the most practical, useful connection to an effective life and a successful organization. Often, it is the most crucial variable in personal and leadership effectiveness. Because purpose is transformational, it converts average-performing organizations, teams, families, and relationships into highly spirited, effective ones. It transforms employees, team members, spouses, or friends into partners. With purpose, managers become leaders. With purpose, however, we not only become leaders of organizations; we become leaders of life.

## EIGHT POINTS FOR PURPOSE MASTERY

Keep the following principles in mind as you begin to master leading with purpose:

*1. Get in Touch with What Is Important to You:* Values are the guideposts to purpose. Understanding what is important, what gives meaning to our lives, is the compass to finding our purpose.

If you have trouble identifying what is really important to you, pay attention to what energizes and excites you, what expands your boundaries and brings you happiness. At various points in your life, you will face a vague sense that there must be something more, some deeper meaning. These are the times you need to dive deep into these experiences to uncover your purpose seeking expression. At these moments, your purpose may be calling, but your lack of listening creates the "vagueness."

**2. Act "On-Purpose":** Most people have an intuitive sense about their purpose in life. Unfortunately, they treat it as a "dream" and never view it as "practical." Following your dream is the most practical thing you can possibly do with your life. But you have to have commitment. Commitment bridges your inner purpose to your outer action. David Prosser, Chairman of RTW, shared with me, "When your commitments are aligned with your purpose, then great things will happen." Committing yourself to pursuing your purpose will marshal energies and potentialities within that you did not know you had. David Whyte explicates, "Take any step toward our destiny through creative action. . . . the universe turns towards us, realizing we are there, alive and about to make our mark." When you face doubts that inhibit you from acting, doubt your doubts and trust your dreams.

**3. Find Team Core Purpose:** While personal purpose is transformative for leaders, team purpose is powerful for the entire enterprise. Once you get clear on how your gifts make a difference, consider engaging your team around a similar exercise. When a team's purpose supports the results drive, great things happen. What is your team's Core Purpose? What are the distinguishing differences your group has? What is the big impact, big service, big difference, you are going to collectively achieve? Imagine a team of leaders clear on their individual Core Purposes and clear on the meaningful connection of their talents and values with their colleagues, with the enterprise, and with their customers. Sound like a great place to be? This could be your team. Connect your individual purpose to the broader mission, and tremendous energy and engagement will be released.

> *Purpose is the still point—the peaceful center around which all dynamic leadership revolves.*
> — Rob Hawthorne

**4. Do Not Mistake the Path for the Goal:** Be careful not to simply adopt other people's views as your purpose. Too often people externalize the latest personal development trend, spiritual teaching, or management guru theory into a dogmatic, inflexible, restrictive practice. This is mistaking the path for the goal. Finding your purpose is finding your essence or calling in life, not just adopting the belief systems of someone else. Personal development programs, religious systems, and great teachers are the paths, the techniques, not the goal. Be careful with programs or systems that impose beliefs onto you, thereby creating more dependency and externalization of the real you. If the process values your uniqueness,

> *Want to lead with purpose? Serve with your whole heart.*
> — Joe Eastman

individuality, and personal path, it may be helpful. Always remind yourself that the program or practice, no matter how stimulating or fulfilling, is the technique—not the goal. The core of Purpose Mastery is discovering how your gifts can serve something bigger than you.

**5. Focus on Service:** Purpose always serves—it is the manner in which we use our gifts to make a difference in the world. Purpose is not purpose without adding value to others. It is not self-expression for its own sake; it is self-expression that creates value for those around you. Therefore, key into your gifts, but don't stop there. Focus on expressing your gifts to improve the lives of everyone and everything you touch.

**6. Be Purposeful in All Domains:** Too often we might be purposeful in one domain of our life and not another. We may be purposeful at work and not so much at home, or we may be purposeful in relationships but not in our work. Once you realize how your gifts can make a difference, then examine the degree to which you are being purposeful in all parts of your life. Seeing these purpose gaps can reveal our growth challenges. Too many purposeful leaders have lost their sense of purpose because they were not using their gifts in their personal lives, or because they were not expressing fully their deepest values in their work. Congruence of purpose in all domains of our life is the aspiration of Purpose Mastery.

**7. Learn from "Failure":** Failure is a subjective label we apply to unintended or unexpected experiences. Usually, we are unwilling or unable to integrate these experiences into a meaningful context. From the vantage point of Purpose Mastery, failure does not exist. It is life attempting to teach us some new lessons or trying to point some new directions. As Warren Bennis wrote in *On Becoming a Leader*, "Everywhere you trip is where the treasure lies." But we have to be open as we "trip." The next time you are experiencing something you didn't intend or expect, ask yourself, "What am I supposed to be learning from this?" When we are living life on-purpose, every life experience helps us to solve the hieroglyphic of meaning. In the words of Emerson, "The world becomes a glass dictionary."

**8. Be Flexible:** Genuine insight into our purpose can be a recurring theme that connects divergent spheres of our lives. Like an orchestra interpreting a symphony, the expression of our purpose will change. For instance, someone's real purpose in life may be to guide and to nurture others. At different stages of the life cycle, this will be expressed very differently—as a child, as a parent, as a professional person, and as a retired person. We need to be flexible, open to the process of expressing our internal sense of purpose in many different roles and life circumstances.

# LEADERSHIP GROWTH PLAN

## PURPOSE MASTERY

It's time to step back, capture some insights and commitments that can make a genuine difference in your life and in your leadership. As you do this, keep asking yourself, "How can I bring forth my talents and values to make a bigger difference?"

1. Areas for Building Awareness:

- _____
- _____
- _____

2. New Commitments to Make:

- _____
- _____
- _____

3. New Practices to Begin:

- _____
- _____
- _____

4. Potential Obstacles:

- _____
- _____
- _____

5. Timeline and Measures of Success:

- _____
- _____
- _____

# CHAPTER THREE

# INTERPERSONAL MASTERY

## *Leading through Synergy and Service*

Martin was an incredibly gifted executive; his talent and intelligence were apparent in everything he did. At early stages of his career his cognitive and intellectual skills helped him to excel in many challenging, complex assignments around the globe. As his achievements advanced, Martin started to believe "his press" and internalized the belief that "he was the person who made things happen at his organization." He began to lose touch with the synergy that was supporting his accomplishments. He thought he was the prime mover, and in reality his teams were the ones creating and supporting his achievements. Gradually his relationships and team dynamics started to become strained, and he couldn't understand why. To help him break through his self-limiting view, we asked him to outline each key event in his life over the past few years by focusing on the people that made each event possible. It didn't take him long to recognize the *web of interdependence that was supporting his success.* He became aware of initiatives for which he had taken credit and for which he now needed to acknowledge others. He was beginning to bridge personal power with synergy power to enhance his contribution.

In a study of 6,403 middle and upper managers conducted by the Foundation for Future Leadership, men and women received their *highest* evaluations for their intellectual competencies. Both groups also received their *lowest* marks for their interpersonal competencies. Although women did score higher than men in communication skills overall, the relative trends were the same. Both groups were highest in their intellectual and their control skills and lowest in their interpersonal skills. This study validates precisely what we've seen while coaching leaders over the past 30 years—leaders must expand their competencies from simply getting results to adding value through collaboration. In their book *The Extraordinary Leader*, John Zenger and Joseph Folkman report research findings based on 400,000 360° assessments that show that the most successful leaders possess multiple strengths or "powerful combinations" of competencies. In their study of combinations of competencies, 66 percent of those leaders in the top quartile for possessing both Focus on Results and Interpersonal

Skills were at the 90th percentile in terms of their overall leadership effectiveness. Meanwhile, 13 percent of leaders with Focus on Results alone were in the 90th percentile, and 9 percent of leaders with Interpersonal Skills alone were at the 90th percentile. These dramatic statistics point us to the following equation: *results competencies plus interpersonal competencies equals top leadership performance.*

## TWO PRINCIPAL STREAMS OF LEADERSHIP DEVELOPMENT

The research of Zenger and Folkman illustrates what we find in the field with our clients globally. There appear to be two main streams of development in leadership. Both approaches are potentially excellent at getting results. One of these leadership approaches is extremely hard-driving and forceful, with a strong sense of personal power—in short, an "I" leader who gets results. These leaders have no problem asserting their power-of-voice (POV), even at the expense of morale at times. This heroic type of leader needs to become more collaborative and relational to bring results to the next level. At times, this kind of hard-driving leadership takes its toll on others. Employees become worn out and drained. They question their purpose and whether or not the money is worth it. This type of leader needs to be more receptive and to develop more authentic connection.

> *Remember that existence consists solely in its possibility for relationships.*
> — Medard Boss

> *If we attach more importance to what other people believe than to what we know to be true—if we value belonging above being—we will not attain authenticity.*
> — Nathaniel Branden

The other leadership approach is more interpersonally connected. These leaders are strongly collaborative and synergistic, and their sense of "We" or power-of-connection (POC) is so strong that they may not appropriately put forth enough of their own power-of-voice ("I") when required. These leaders need to become more forceful and courageous in expressing their authentic influence.

In organizations there is an underground debate going on, or what might be called a cultural battle, between proponents of one stream of leadership or the other. Some say that we need more hard-edged, performance-driven, "I"-oriented leaders, who assert their power-of-voice to get more results. On the other side of the debate, people assert that we need more of the "We"-oriented, team-oriented leadership to get more performance. They say we would be better off if the hard-edged, driving leaders would just step back and connect more. Based on research and what we see with our clients, there is really no basis for this debate. If we aspire to genuine, world-class leadership, we need to develop both streams, power-of-voice—"I"—and power-of-connection—"We." Zenger and Folkman's research made this very clear. If we are weighted too strongly in our personal and performance power, we have to work on the "We." Ideally, we can flex the "I" muscle when we feel it is needed to express a strong point of view and the "We" muscle when it is needed to enhance the connection needed to sustain performance. What do you need to do more of, less of, or differently regarding these two streams of development? Do you need to develop more "I" or more "We?"

Interpersonal Mastery is also about balancing our courageous influence, our voice, with human connection. This is not easy. As a matter of fact, it is one of the most difficult leadership challenges. When we perceive two powerful elements—our power-of-voice and our power-of-connection or acceptance by others—coming together, we experience one of our easier leadership moments. The harder ones come when we have to spend some relational equity. We risk or give up acceptance and popularity to assert our voice . . . our authentic influence. This requires exceptional courage because we are giving up something that is important to us for what we believe is more important over time. At these very difficult moments, if our "I"—personal power—is not courageous enough, we may withhold our voice. As you go through the book, notice which type of leader you are. Do you need to develop more "I"? Or, do you need to develop more "we"? The examples in the book deal with both of these leadership dynamics. The following story, which really happened to a friend of David Whyte, and is similar to Dr. Jerry B. Harvey's *Abilene Paradox*, illustrates the challenges even very senior leaders face when it comes to speaking up with a more powerful voice.

David's friend, an executive and member of a senior team, decided he was ready to retire from a successful corporate career. His reputation was intact. Financially, he was in great shape. By all measures he was all set. His CEO had a pet project that was important to him, but he was frustrated by his senior team because they didn't seem to support it. The truth was they didn't think the project had value, and they hoped, if they kept avoiding it, he would forget about it. He didn't. Instead, one day he called his senior team into the conference room and said, "Okay. I want to hear from each of you about this project. On a scale of 1 to 10, 10 meaning you are fully behind the strategy and 1 meaning you are against it." He turned to the first person and said, "Okay. What do you think?" David's friend thought, "Wow! Now the CEO is going to get some real feedback." But to his surprise and disappointment,

> *One need ask only one question, "What for? What am I to unify my being for?" The reply is: Not for my own sake.*
>
> — Martin Buber

the first team member said, "Ten, Bob." The next said, "Ten, Bob." The next "brave" soul said, "Nine and a half, Bob." When the CEO got all the way around the table to David's friend, he said, in a squeaky, hesitant, mouse-like voice, "Ten, Bob."

All of us do "Ten, Bobs." But these are the real-time courageous moments of leadership when we step forward or step back. If we step forward, we align our voice, our values, and our experience in a manner that creates value. It is in these everyday moments of leadership when we either choose to do that or we choose not to. Can we be courageous, authentic, and in alignment when doing so is not popular? What have been your "Ten, Bob moments?" What are the situations that most inhibit your authentic voice?

Culture—both corporate and societal—influences us powerfully from the outside-in toward the "I" or the "We" leadership approaches. Both approaches have an upside and a downside. Just as the tough, results-dominated culture has its downside or shadow consequences, so does the culture that supports too much niceness and politeness. These companies are pleasant, wonderful places to work. But the shadow is that people may be overly nice or passive-aggressive. Often, they avoid the tough conversations and constructive conflict. Authentic influence may be sacrificed on the alter of niceness. As a result, individual points of view may not come forward, and innovation may be compromised.

It is crucial to build your awareness regarding your own strengths and development needs here. Do you need to develop more voice or more connection—more "I" or more "We"? From what vantage point do you typically lead—"I" or "We"? What is the culture asking of your behavior—more "I" or more "We"? Our responses to these questions may be the same or they may be different. We need to reconcile both streams of leadership, the "I" and the "We," with the inside-out and outside-in dynamic. Do we need more connection or more personal power? What is the environment around us asking for more of from the outside-in? What is your heart telling you from the inside-out? *World-class leadership operates at the dynamic junction of personal authenticity and interpersonal connection.*

## BUILDING RELATIONSHIP BRIDGES

Relationships are the bridges that connect authenticity to influence and value creation. Leadership is not influence for its own sake; it's influence that makes a difference, that enriches the lives of others. Leadership does not exist in a vacuum. It always operates in context, in relationship. *While leaders may lead by virtue of who they are, leaders also create value by virtue of their relationships.* As the chairman of a global technology services firm shared with me, "Leadership is not about sitting in your office and dreaming up strategy; it is about touching the organization through personal presence and relationship."

As crucial as relationships are to leadership success, many of us, like Martin, have a difficult time breaking out of the self-limiting illusion that we are "the ones that make things happen." All too often, successful, achievement-oriented people mistakenly believe they are the prime movers, the origin of accomplishments in their groups or organizations. Most leaders would not admit to this, but often their behavior clearly demonstrates this tendency. Research by the Saratoga Institute makes a startling case for the consequences of poor interpersonal skills. The Institute interviewed 19,700 people—exiting employees and their bosses. The results indicated that 85 percent of bosses said that their former employees left for more compensation and opportunity. On the other hand, 80 percent of the exiting employees said they left because of poor relationship, poor development, and poor coaching from the boss. Neil Anthony, Senior Vice President of Human Resources for Novartis Pharmaceuticals, emphasized this key interpersonal skill this way, "Coaching others—particularly coaching upward—is one of the most critical interpersonal competencies for senior leaders today. It multiplies impact, accelerates development, clarifies strategy, and transmits values."

Unfortunately, many driven leaders fail to comprehend how nothing is accomplished without engaging in relationships and appreciating the unique contribution of many, many people. Some leaders even feel slowed down or frustrated by the teaming or synergy process. Lawrence Perlman, former Chairman and CEO of Ceridian, sees it differently: "Leadership will not add enough value if it only comes from the top—it needs to come from the very guts of the business itself to make a meaningful and enduring difference."

It has been interesting to chart the high-growth, low-pitch success of Taiwanese computer maker Acer, Inc. In contrast to the glamorous competition usually associated with computer sales, Acer has gone quietly about its business and is now nipping at the heels of Dell to become the world's second biggest notebook seller. Certainly, a good share of the credit goes to the company's president, Gianfranco Lanci, the son of an Italian construction worker, who has become the first non-Asian ever to hold such high rank among Taiwan's technology titans. Lanci, the understated yet upbeat company president, always flies business class and is an anomaly compared to the razzle-dazzle of most fast-moving high-tech execs. Yet, as

*Forbes Asia* pointed out last year, the unconventional leader headquartering out of a foreign culture where he barely speaks the language has somehow found success by winning over Acer's 5,300 employees because he "beams humility" and "treasures relationships." Amid a landscape of headlines related to more heroic, charismatic styles of leadership, it may be easy to point to cultural factors as a key reason for Lanci's management success. In reality, though, he's at the forefront of an emerging approach to global leadership. Jim Collins in *Good to Great* calls individuals like Lanci "Level 5 Leaders," and once referred to them as "tofu leaders: leaders who are somewhat bland, mix really well with everything around them, and provide lots of sustenance and value." Perhaps a more heroic, take-no-prisoners approach is needed in some business environments, but today sustaining leaders must be able to blend people effectiveness with their affinity for results. My colleague Bob Eichinger, Co-Founder of Lominger International, the world expert in leadership competencies, adds that interpersonal skills are what separate high-performing leaders from the rest of the pack. "The key difference between good leaders and legacy leaders is not only about results; it's about their people competencies. Legacy leaders are the orchestra conductors. They get the right people in the right chairs. They structure the score. They connect the score and the people. They make it happen by bringing it all together."

Besides not being the only prime movers of our organizations, as leaders we must admit very little of what we know can be said to be really our own. Our language, culture, education, and beliefs have all come to us through others. We have acquired them through relationships. James Flaherty, author of *Evoking Excellence in Others,* has personally taught me this key principle: Those who say they are truly "self-made leaders" are ignoring many generations of people before them, and they lack the confidence and character to learn from and give credit to others.

> *Life's most urgent question is, "What are you doing for others?"*
> — Martin Luther King, Jr.

## BALANCING PERSONAL POWER WITH SYNERGY POWER AND CONTRIBUTION POWER

One of the crucial development challenges for most leaders is learning how to authentically influence in a manner that creates value. This is not to say that leaders are not getting results—they usually are. What is missing are results that are adding value and contribution at the same time. How often do leaders get results but leave a wake of bodies in the process? How often do businesses get results and leave people or the environment damaged? This is getting results without creating value, without making an enduring contribution. This is getting results at the expense of, rather than in service of, many relationships or constituencies.

A while ago, I had the good fortune to be able to sit down and talk with John Dalla Costa, author of *The Ethical Imperative*. While I shared my song and dance on leadership, I was dying to ask John, "What the heck is ethics?" At the appropriate moment, I sprang the question. To my surprise, John's answer was succinct: "Ethics is others." I thought, "That's it? Twenty-five years of research and the answer is three small words?" Later, as I let John's concentrated wisdom sink in, the profound simplicity and complexity of his definition hit me. Leaders face ethical dilemmas every day, and it usually boils down to people—managing constant stakeholder-related trade-offs and serving one constituency better or more than another. Every day we are to some degree ethical and to some degree unethical. We can't make failsafe decisions on a regular basis, but we can be aware of how we impact others by our choices.

Ken Melrose, former Toro Chairman and CEO, shared with me one of the company's ethical dilemmas, which centered around a lawnmower product that had become a new commercial market standard. The product, unique because it turns on a dime, has a very low center of gravity. Consequently, it is very hard to overturn; but in the rare instance that it does overturn, it flips over 180° and can seriously injure the operator. While the mower met compliance standards, Toro decided to add a roll bar behind the seat as an added safety precaution without raising the price on newly manufactured units. As the company further considered the needs of "others," Toro faced another tough decision. What about existing units? Don't they deserve the same ethical treatment? The initial, Pollyanna answer was yes, but the strict financial answer was no. After all, auto companies didn't retrofit all used cars with seatbelts, and if Toro did install the roll bar on used machines, another constituent, shareholders, would be adversely affected. So, what was the right thing to do? Was an old customer as valuable as a new one, or as important as shareholders, who may have invested much more of themselves into the company? Melrose's company installed the roll bars for all machines, new and old, at their own cost. They reasoned that although the decision was a costly one for shareholders immediately, they had made a value-creating decision that served both customers and investors for the long haul. Seeing the longer-term consequences to all constituents—to all the "others"—Toro made a tough, ethical leadership decision.

As leaders, we need to make this crucial development shift by balancing our personal power (authentic influence) with synergy power and contribution power (creating value). If we

*Success is going from failure to failure without loss of enthusiasm.*
— Winston Churchill

attempt to use our personal power to achieve results while ignoring synergy power—a common dominant, driven leadership style—real contribution and a people-centered culture are sacrificed on the altar of immediate achievement. In their discussion of "Intentional Work" in the book *Presence: An Exploration of Profound Change in People, Organizations, and Society*, Peter Senge and his co-authors say, "When people in leadership positions begin to serve a vision infused with a larger purpose, their work shifts naturally from producing results to encouraging the growth of people who produce results." Most organizations today take a very mechanistic approach to this model. Many companies tend to focus on results at all costs and drive the organization and people to support these goals.

*We're all in this together, by ourselves!*
— Lily Tomlin

This mechanistic approach prizes results over synergy and synergy over the individual. It's an outside-in view of organizations and people. This approach to leading organizations leaves people feeling devalued and wondering, "Where do I fit in? Why am I here?" It's an approach to leadership that misses the power of human engagement. An organic, as opposed to mechanistic, approach to business sees people as the source of creativity and dynamism. In this type of organization, personal power supports synergy power, which in turn contributes something of value to multiple constituencies: customers, employees, and the environment. This inside-out model of organizations creates a purposeful culture where people are constantly thinking, "How can I make more of a contribution? How can I apply my gifts with others to make a difference?" It's a purposeful, dynamic approach to organizational leadership that values and leverages the power of human aspiration.

Unfortunately, many leaders are limiting their effectiveness by using only their personal power to drive for results. In the process they have adopted a tough, get-it-done persona—devoid of much emotional intelligence or sustained performance. Winning at all costs rules the day, and relationships are seen as a means to an end—getting the results. Unknowingly, sustainable results are being compromised on a long-term basis because the collaborative power of the organization declines.

A while ago, I spoke to a CEO who had started to build his bridge from personal power to relational power. After a long struggle "to set his organization right," he finally had to change his approach and value the power of synergy. Describing his experience, he told me, "My rules just weren't working anymore. The more I tried to assert my will, the worse things got. Not only was I attempting to take total responsibility for the turnaround, I also was taking the total blame for any problems. I was amazingly self-centered. I believed the fate of the entire business was mine alone. Letting go of that belief freed me to really lead us to a new future." Peter Block, in his book *Stewardship,* wrote, "We are reluctant to let go of the belief that 'if I am to care for something, I must control it.' "

Paul Walsh, Chairman and CEO of Diageo, described it to me this way: "As managers, we are trained as cops who are supposed to keep things under control. As leaders, we need to shift from control to trust." Giving an apt description of balancing personal power with synergy power, he went on to say, "I don't care who you are or how great you are, no one person can totally claim the victory or totally abstain from the defeat." Learning to move our belief from thinking "I have all the answers" to "together we have all the answers" is the first crucial step in Interpersonal Mastery.

## REDUCING THE INTENTION-PERCEPTION GAP

The second step for leaders is to realize that we often lack full awareness of our impact on others. We assume to an amazing degree that other people clearly and fully receive our intended communication. It's a *huge* leap of faith that does not hold up under sufficient investigation. Have you ever had a great laugh with a group of people and then asked each person what they thought was so funny? Probably you were surprised to discover the unique perspective from which each person interprets the world.

All of us have been communicating our intentions since we delivered our first kick in our mother's womb. Since then, our rich, well-practiced internal conversations have evolved considerably, and we take for granted that others are receiving precisely our intended meaning. We express ourselves, and then we are shocked when our messages are misunderstood. Emerson wrote: "Men imagine that they communicate their virtue or vice only by overt actions, and do not see that virtue or vice emit a breath every moment."

Becoming skilled at receiving feedback from others becomes crucial to ensure that our imprint is beneficial to others. Effective leadership requires us to constantly reduce the gap between intended and perceived communication. As one CEO likes to remind me, "I always start with API—Assumption of Positive Intent. Ninety-nine point nine percent of the leaders I know want to do well for themselves and others." Although most leaders have good intentions, the way others on all levels of the organization receive their intentions can be quite diverse.

## BEYOND 360° FEEDBACK TO 720° FEEDBACK

The tool most organizations use to help leaders deal with the intention-perception gap is 360° feedback. With such programs, leaders are given feedback from multiple sources on their behavior, skills, and leadership approaches.

Unfortunately, 360° feedback does not reveal the full horizon. From a development perspective, it reveals only a portion of the person, rather than a total picture. This is particularly true when 360° feedback is the sole source of self-understanding given to the leader. If a development process is modeled primarily around 360° feedback, executives only learn how to create themselves in the image of others. As a result, they learn how to act instead of how to be—a direct route to following vs. leading. In a provocative way, I tell most of my client organizations, "You don't need 360° feedback. What you need for your leaders is *720° Feedback*." After they give me a polite, somewhat confused stare, I elaborate that 360° feedback in the absence of new self-knowledge often has two limitations:

> *If you are irritated by every rub, how will your mirror be polished?*
>
> — Rumi

1. It can create a defensive reaction, and therefore no growth takes place.
2. It encourages people to simply deliver the desired behaviors without giving them the personal insight and motivation to grow—a formula destined to limit authentic influence by creating actors vs. leaders.

But *720° Feedback* is different. It begins with an *Inside-Out 360*—a deep, broad, well-integrated understanding of ourselves, as well as our current and desired stages of development. This first stage ensures that we begin to master a more authentic understanding of ourselves. Then, an *Outside-In 360* is completed to give broad feedback on how people above, across, and below us perceive our strengths and areas of development. With *720° Feedback*, leaders now have a complete context to reconcile their inner and outer realities.

For instance, I worked with a vice president of a consumer products company, who prior to our coaching received 360° feedback from his company. He was perceived as too aggressive and untrustworthy. He was devastated by the feedback because he lacked the self-knowledge to meaningfully interpret the harsh input. He had no idea what to do. Should he pull back on his relationships and be less aggressive? If he did that, wouldn't it further erode his sense of trust with people? Since he didn't know himself at a deep enough level, he was unable to assimilate the feedback, and he was totally paralyzed developmentally.

After completing our *Executive to Leader Institute* and getting an integrated *720°* view of himself, his entire situation clarified. For the first time, he became objectively aware that he was extremely aggressive and dominant. He had no idea his interpersonal style was so far beyond the norm for leaders. Suddenly he had a context to understand the value of this part of the feedback, and he was motivated to show up in a manner more consistent with his real intentions. Regarding the trustworthiness factor, we found in the *Inside-Out 360* that he was a very honest person of high integrity. However, his somewhat introverted, aloof approach with people was creating a perception that he held things back. Knowing this, the challenge was of a different order. He needed to spend more time with relationships across from him to let people get to know him. Once he got the complete *720° Feedback*, he was able to engage actively in a development plan to move forward.

## INTIMATE CONNECTION OF PERSONAL MASTERY AND INTERPERSONAL MASTERY

As we discussed earlier in the book, mastery of *leadership from the inside out* is about consciously making a difference by fully applying our talents. This does not mean that we lead only from the inside-out. On the contrary, we lead just as much from the outside-in. Leadership is a constant dynamic between the inner and the outer and vice versa. We are in a continuing flow, a dynamic relationship with ourselves and our constituencies—the marketplace, our customers, our employees, our personal relationships. Ultimately, we want a balance of leading from the inside-out and the outside-in. Our decisions and actions are in a dynamic loop from us to others and back again. To practice leadership at the highest level, we need to be equally vigilant about both the "I" and the "We" in effective leadership.

Therefore, in addition to using *720° Feedback* as a best practice, it is also important to get feedback in real time. As you are interacting with others, are you watching for cues of discomfort, misunderstanding, or inappropriate silence from people? Ask people for their feedback on your views and how you are coming across. Even if you are quite sure people are listening, ask them what they think. Encourage people to challenge you. Ask people if there are other ways to view this. Don't assume. Make sure they have received your intentions. If not, ask them what they heard, and then take the time to clarify until you are satisfied your intentions have been received. This will serve a threefold purpose:

1. Your influence will be even more authentic and create more value.

2. You will learn more about how you are being perceived.

3. You will develop more effective ways to communicate.

In the 2006 edition of Lominger's *100 Things You Need to Know: Best People Practices for Managers & HR*, Eichinger, Lombardo, and Ulrich report results of a study showing that "although it might seem mildly counterintuitive, high potentials, and especially executives, get less feedback. They are more likely to be told how wonderfully they are doing; specific feedback or even formal performance appraisals can be rare." Don't let yourself fall into this trap. Make *720°* and real-time feedback a way to accelerate your self-awareness and interpersonal awareness.

## OPENING UP POSSIBILITIES

I was driving around Lake Calhoun in Minneapolis on a brilliant spring day. As you may know, spring in Minneapolis is dramatic and transformative. From the depths of winter, everything explodes into life. Seemingly all at once, the trees bloom and the birds return. As I was driving along appreciating all of this, a big fat robin flew into the front grille of my car and was killed immediately. I pulled over to check it out, and there was nothing I could do. As I drove away, I started to think that just a moment ago this beautiful bird had been enjoying her life, tending to her family, fulfilling her purpose. In a flash, I came along and unintentionally shut all of that down. How often do we do that in our relationships? How often as leaders do we come barreling through our organizations and shut others down? If we are honest, we will admit that we all do it more often than we care to imagine. Shutting people down instead of opening them up can occur in what seems like the most innocent, meaningless ways. Leaders need to be a more well rounded breed of corporate athlete with "people muscles" ready to bend and flex just as much as "results muscles" under more diverse and challenging circumstances.

> *Leaders must attend to one key growth question: How authentically am I showing up in the world and in my organization?*
>
> — Tom Gegax

Practicing Interpersonal Mastery isn't easy, and it takes time. We don't always feel we have the time to pause and listen. When I return from lengthy business trips, I want to return to the office to "get things done." My first internal reaction to colleagues walking into my office is, "Yeah, what do you want?" But the important interpersonal discipline is to move away from my keyboard and my "busyness" and be present with them for a few minutes. The results part of me feels like I just slowed down, but this is eventually counterbalanced by the people part of me that knows I just gave someone else fuel to go faster. Marilyn Carlson Nelson, one of *Fortune*'s "50 Most Powerful Women in Business" and CEO of Carlson Companies, one of the largest privately held corporations in the United States, expressed this perspective in an interview with a Carlson School of Management publication: "Employees who feel that their management cares about them as a person, in return care about the organization for which they work. And isn't that the key to a successful enterprise?"

## THE POTENTIALLY TRANSFORMING POWER OF PRESENCE

I'm sure we've all been in the presence of a great leader who has the extraordinary power to walk into a room and fill the room with energy and connection. Many people have commented that John F. Kennedy, Mahatma Gandhi, Nelson Mandela, Bill Clinton, and other leaders have this extraordinary ability. Some time ago, I was coaching someone who was very vocal about his lack of support for former President Clinton. During this period, my client's daughters heard about Hurricane Katrina and decided to do something to help. They designed a Web site about the crisis with a vision to collect one dollar from every student in the United States. The Web site caught on like wildfire, and the girls raised tens of thousands of dollars. Bill Clinton heard about their success, contacted the girls, and said that he wanted to meet with them while he was visiting Minneapolis. Excited, the girls listened to the arrangements and looked forward to being there with their parents. At a coaching session before the meeting, my client complained, "Oh, no! Now I have to meet with the guy!" Grudgingly, he took his daughters to the airport, and they waited at the designated meeting place for the former president's private jet to land. From the moment the jet's doorway opened and Bill Clinton stepped out, his eyes locked onto the two girls. He greeted them by their first names, conversed knowledgeably about their Web site, and praised their work with genuine enthusiasm and appreciation. He showered them with his complete attention, and during that brief meeting the two girls felt as if they were the only two people in the world that mattered. It was a transformative moment for all of them, including my client, who said at his next coaching session, "I still don't like his politics, but he is amazing as a person."

Presence is an amazing quality. Not only because it draws our attention to the individual who exudes it, but because its power can inspire and energize the potential of those in its

*They must often change who would be constant in happiness or wisdom.*
— Confucius

midst. Who knows what that transformative moment may have meant to the girls? Perhaps it will influence their academic choices, their service, and their career paths. We don't have to be president, prime minister, or statesman of a nation to exude presence. Taking the time to give those around us our undivided attention, as well as our authentic listening and appreciation, is a way to cultivate this powerful, transformative ability.

## MOVING FROM LEADER TO OPENER

One of the most crucial qualities of character in a leader is openness—openness to new possibilities in the marketplace, openness to new learnings and strategies, openness to relationships, openness to new ways of doing things, openness to encouraging people to pursue possibilities. It's so important to leadership, maybe we should stop calling people "leaders" and rename them "openers." Leaders open up or shut down opportunities in direct proportion to how open or shut down they are to themselves.

We worked with a senior executive a while ago who sincerely believed in openness. What he didn't realize was that his way of being direct and frank with people was actually shutting them down. He believed in openness and authenticity, but his approach was creating the opposite effect. It was a total mystery to him. He even rationalized it by saying that other people in his organization just weren't as open as he was. What was missing was openness to himself. He could be open and direct when it came to driving people to results or expressing criticism. He could not be open about his fears, limitations, inadequacies, or vulnerabilities. As a result, his embodiment of "openness" was very limited. Once he gained the inner strength and confidence to be more open about his real concerns and feelings in situations, it came as a great surprise to him how other people then opened up to him. He told me, "It was startling to me that people opened up and supported me as I opened up and shared my vulnerabilities. I built my career by being invulnerable. I was very open about the work, but very fearful about revealing myself. I didn't understand that I was distancing people in the process. I now understand that more openness in the organization begins with me."

Anne Morrow Lindbergh wrote, "When one is a stranger to oneself, then one is estranged from others, too. If one is out of touch with oneself, then one cannot touch others." As a world-class international consultant, Suzanne really touched her clients. When asked why her clients had such outstanding regard for her, she quickly replied, "I treat each one with the respect and service of an honored guest. I feel privileged to be associated with them and want them to feel served. I can't fully explain it; I just treat them like a guest in my home." Unfortunately, Suzanne's co-workers reported that they did not feel like guests. They felt that Suzanne only cared about "looking special" in her clients' eyes and cared very little about them. Suzanne was not aware of her excessive need to "be special." This need was generated by her Shadow Belief "I'm not good enough as I am." As a result, Suzanne was driven to validate her uniqueness from the outside. Once she understood this dynamic and comprehended emotionally how mistreated her co-workers felt, she was very motivated to treat everyone in her life as "guests." She worked on her limiting beliefs and changed her relationship paradigm from self-service to service-to-others.

## TRUSTING AND ENGAGING IN CONSTRUCTIVE CONFLICT

In helping senior teams to elevate their game to the next level, we consistently find two crucial areas in need of development: trust and constructive conflict. Teams that can authentically face these two interpersonal challenges can accelerate performance greatly.

Following the merger of a major consumer products firm, a newly forming team came face to face with these two major issues. While they acted very friendly and cordial to each other on the surface, the truth was the group members really did not trust each other. Consequently, they did not have the *courage and relationship to engage openly and honestly or to have constructive conflict*. As a result, they generated no new innovative strategies and they relied on a series of fast executions. The business pace became sluggish, falling directly in step with the low level of trust and engagement holding back the senior team. As is common with most senior teams, team members retreated to the comforts of their function or business unit to do the "real work." In our *LeaderSynergy*® team process with them, we needed to create a forum for these people to build relationship, get to know each other, forge a purpose bigger than their concern for themselves, gain the tools to have positive conflict, and eventually, build trust. An undertaking like this is much more than an off-site event. We worked through this process—individually and collectively—over several months. Slowly our meetings warmed up. With respect and understanding, leaders began to challenge each other. Individual leaders committed to coaching sessions to get ready to show up in new ways. The CEO embodied new behaviors and "walked the talk" of the new values and purpose expressed by the team. After nine months, our measures of trust increased by 60 percent, and over 12 months by 76 percent. Dealing with conflict constructively improved by 43 percent. The team had internalized Interpersonal Mastery at a new and rewarding level.

Commenting on the value of team development from the inside out, Bruce Nicholson, CEO of Thrivent Financial, shared, "Going beyond the typical event-driven, team-building session to a real inside-out process involving deep individual coaching and meaningful group dynamics work is the key to impacting simultaneously personal, interpersonal, and business growth." Real team development involves integrated Personal Mastery, Interpersonal Mastery, and Business/Strategic Mastery—all in one process.

# REFLECTION

## BUILDING RELATIONSHIPS

Take some time to increase your awareness of how to develop and to build relationships more effectively as a leader by reflecting on the following questions:

1. Under what conditions do you shut down communication?

2. What beliefs are causing you to shut down?

3. How can you be more open in future situations?

4. How can you move from the "I" to the "We" of leadership more often?

5. What personal beliefs are causing you to hold back?

6. How can you be more open and influential?

7. How can you more effectively build your relationship bridges?

8. How can you bring your team trust and team effectiveness to a new level?

## SIX POINTS FOR AUTHENTIC INTERPERSONAL MASTERY

Authenticity is the core of relationships around which synergy and trust grow. Imagine a relationship without authenticity. Can it survive? Certainly not long term. Authenticity is the life force of relationships; it is the true voice of the leader as it touches other people's hearts. From observing the most effective leaders, I would suggest there are Six Points for Authentic Interpersonal Mastery which bridge genuine influence to value creation.

> *The most important thing in communication is to hear what isn't being said.*
> — Peter Drucker

**1. Know Yourself Authentically:** Throughout the ages the phrase *nosce teipsum,* know thyself, appears over and over in the writings of Ovid, Cicero, and Socrates, in the sayings of the Seven Sages of Greece, on the entrance to the temple of Apollo, in Christian writings, and in Eastern texts. One scholar says it was part of Shakespeare's "regular moral and religious diet."

*Nosce teipsum* threads its way through history as the pre-eminent precept in life. Chaucer: "Full wise is he that can himself know." Browning: "Trust is within ourselves." Pope: "And all our knowledge is, ourselves to know." Montaigne: "If a man does not know himself, how should he know his functions and his powers?" de Saint-Exupéry: "Each man must look to himself to teach him the meaning of life." Lao Tzu: "Knowledge of self is the source of our abilities."

Contemporary thinkers from Ralph Waldo Emerson to Abraham Maslow to Warren Bennis have carried on the tradition. Emerson wrote, "The purpose of life seems to be to acquaint man with himself." Bennis writes: "Letting the self emerge is the essential task of leaders." If we want to be more effective with others, we first need to become more effective with ourselves. Instead of focusing on finding the right partner (in business or friendships), seek to be the right partner. Commit to getting to know your total self authentically through Personal Mastery. Practice being what you wish others to become.

**2. Listen Authentically:** How often are we truly present with someone? How often do we pause, set aside all our concerns—past, present, and future—and completely "be there" for someone else? How often do we really hear what the other person is saying and feeling vs. filtering it heavily through our own immediate concerns and time pressures? Authentic listening is not easy. We hear the words, but rarely do we really listen. We hear the words, but do we also "hear" the emotions, fears, underlying concerns? Authentic listening is not a technique. It is centered in presence and in a concern for the other person that goes beyond our self-centered needs. Listening authentically is centered in the principle of psychological reciprocity: to influence others, we must first be open to their influence. Authentic listening is the attempt, as St. Francis said, "To understand first and be understood second." It places the other person's self-expression as primary at that moment. Authentic listening is about being generous—listening with a giving attitude that seeks to bring forth the contribution in someone vs. listening with our limiting assessments, opinions, and judgments. Authentic listening is about being open to the purpose and learning coming to us through the other person.

Listening is not the same as waiting for the other person to finish speaking. I find it amusing to observe leaders who think that not speaking is the same as really listening. Fidgeting in their chairs and doing several things at once, many leaders give numerous, simultaneous cues that they are anywhere but present with people. One successful senior executive I was about to coach on how others perceived his poor listening skills was so agitated while listening to me, he actually threw his pen across the room. His impatience and inner distress were so strong, he couldn't even listen to me for a minute without his "dis-ease" bursting through his body and making him fling his Montblanc across my office! It was a very embarrassing moment for him to see precisely what other people witnessed in his behavior.

Try practicing authentic listening. Be with people and have the goal to fully understand the thoughts and feelings they are trying to express. Use your questions and comments to draw them out, to open them up, and to clarify what is said vs. expressing your view, closing them down, and saying only what you want. Not only will this help you to understand what value and contribution the other person has, it will create a new openness in the relationship that will allow you to express yourself more authentically, as well.

Authentic listening creates the platform for true synergy and team effectiveness. Being open to valuing and attending to different perspectives from diverse sources results in a more complete understanding of issues and more authentic solutions. Research clearly has identified communication skills as core to leadership effectiveness, and listening skills are the core of communication. Authentic listening is the soul of synergy.

**3. Influence Authentically:** Authentic influence is a delicate subject for many leaders. I have yet to meet a leader who would admit readily that he or she lacks some degree of integrity. I also have yet to meet a leader who has complete integrity in all parts of his or her life.

Integrity goes far beyond telling the truth. Integrity means total congruence between who we are and what we do. It is a formidable goal, and most of us will spend our lifetime on the path to getting there. How often have we held back something that we feel is important because we are fearful of expressing it? How often have we expressed something in a slightly more favorable light? How often have we protected someone from what we consider a tough message? How often have we feigned modesty for something we were really proud of?

> *If A is success in life, then A equals X plus Y plus Z. Work is X, Y is play and Z is keeping your mouth shut.*
> — Albert Einstein

Authentic influence is the true voice of the leader. We speak it from our character, and it creates trust, synergy, and connection with everyone around us. Authentic influence is *not* simply refining our presentation style—it's deeper than that. Some of the most authentic leaders I know stumble around a bit in their delivery, but the words come right from their hearts and experiences. You can feel it. You feel their conviction and the integral connection of who they are and what they say. Benjamin Franklin wrote, "Think innocently and justly, and, if you speak, speak accordingly."

Authentic influence is about straight talk that creates value. It's not about hurting people with bluntness or insensitivity. Expressing yourself authentically is sharing your real thoughts and feelings in a manner that opens up possibilities. It's not about delivering only positive messages and avoiding the negatives—sometimes the most difficult messages can open up the most possibilities if shared in a thoughtful, compassionate manner. Influencing authentically is what one CEO I know calls "caring confrontation"—the unique blending of straight talk with a genuine concern for people. Like many leaders, my CEO friend had been uncomfortable with such interaction for years. As his career progressed, he realized, "Real caring involves giving people the tough feedback they need to grow." Al Schuman, former President and CEO of Ecolab, supports this view: "A leader's ability to be appropriately tough is directly proportional to the depth and quality of his or her relationships." Carl Jung said it this way: "To confront a person in his shadow is to show him his light."

Start observing how authentically you are expressing yourself. How are you doing with your requests and with your promises? Fernando Flores, communication expert and President of Business Design Associates, boiled down his powerful communication paradigm to this: "A human society operates through the expression of requests and promises." Are you authentically expressing your requests? Are you authentically fulfilling your promises? Use this model as a guide to authentic influence; it is very transformative.

In other areas of expressing yourself authentically, are you adding a positive spin here or withholding something there? How can you effectively deliver a tough message to someone with warmth and concern? Are you willing to risk revealing your fears and vulnerabilities to express how you are really feeling? If you commit to expressing authenticity, you will not come away from relationships the same as you went in—you will come away having opened up possibilities and having created new value.

*4. Appreciate Authentically:* As leaders, we do too much and appreciate too little. Has anyone ever appreciated you too much? It would probably be safe to say that human beings have an infinite capacity to be appreciated. Lenny Bruce wrote, "There are never enough 'I love you's.'" A mentor of mine once told me, "Love is an extreme case of appreciation." However, as leaders we don't appreciate enough, much less love enough. In fact, we have banned the "L" word from business. In spite of the fact that the "L" word is the substance that unifies teams, builds cultures, fosters commitment, and bonds people to an organization, it is not socially acceptable even to say the "L" word in a business context. We can say we hate someone with no repercussions, but if we say we love someone, we may be banished for life! In lieu of this cultural taboo, let's use the word "appreciation." Appreciation is one type of influence that creates value. It energizes people and makes people want to exceed their goals and perceived limits. Criticism is one type of influence that usually does not add value. What it typically adds is fear and insecurity. Criticism may get some short-term results, but a constant dosage tends to be toxic. Judging others critically doesn't define them anyway, it defines us. An Islamic aphorism suggests, "A thankful person is thankful under all circumstances. A complaining soul complains even if he lives in paradise."

As leaders, we need to follow the advice of William Penn: "If there is any kindness I can show, or any good thing I can do to any fellow being, let me do it now, and not deter or neglect it, as I shall not pass this way again." What would an organization or team be like if people willingly expressed this type of appreciation for one another?

Studies done by John Gottmann and described in his book *Why Marriages Succeed and Why Marriages Fail,* found that relationships that had a 5 to 1 ratio of appreciation to criticism were thriving, healthy, and productive. However, relationships that were at a 1 to 1 ratio of appreciation to criticism were doomed to failure. Divorces were the inevitable result of falling to a 1 to 1 ratio or lower.

Practice appreciating authentically. Look for what is going well—point it out and have some fun celebrating the good things as they come up. Shift your analysis of situations from finding fault to finding the value being added. Move from critic to coach. As Thomas Ebeling, CEO of Novartis Consumer and Pharmaceutical groups, shared with me, "Moving from critic to coach as a leader may be one of the most powerful tools we have as leaders to generate energy, engagement, enthusiasm, and results in an organization. It is at the core of transformational leadership." Acknowledge effort and intention even if the results are occasionally lacking. Trust that your appreciation will energize people. Commit to a culture of acknowledgement and appreciation—have team members commit to being a source of acknowledgement and appreciation to one another. Learn to give, receive, and encourage generously abundant appreciation. Appreciation transmits energy, and as Emerson wrote, "The world belongs to the energetic." Multiply your leadership energy through the practice of genuine appreciation.

> *Appreciation is a wonderful thing. It makes what is excellent in others belong to us as well.*
>
> — Voltaire

**5. Share Stories Authentically:** Stories are the language of leadership. They separate a boring, personally detached, closed manager from a motivating, personally connected, open leader. Real power emanates from our ability to connect to ourselves and those around us. That is the power and universality of classics, stories that regardless of their time or their place, connect us emotionally to themes, characters, and conflicts that are still relevant today. Through personal connection, ideas take shape and develop energy, moving from thoughts and feelings out into the world and then back again. The energy is circular. Your real-life personal or career stories are inspiring tools for building this kind of energy and relationship bridge. "To communicate is not just a matter of pushing information at another person," Daniel Goleman said. "It's creating an experience, to engage their emotional gut and that's an emotional craft." Craft authentic stories to bring your values to life and to build deeper emotional connection with your people.

**6. Serve Authentically:** As a very wise, 80-year-old CEO shared with me, "I think one of the key questions every leader must ask himself or herself is, 'How do I want to be of service to others?' " Ultimately, a leader is not judged so much by how well he or she leads, but by how well he or she serves. All value and contribution are achieved through service. Do we have any other purpose in life but to serve? As leaders, we may think we're "leading," but in reality we're serving. Leadership is a continuum of service. We serve our organization. We serve our people. We serve our customers. We serve our marketplace. We serve our community. We serve our family. We serve our relationships. At the heart of service is the principle of interdependence: relationships are effective when mutual benefits are served.

Capturing the essence of serving authentically, Peter Block writes in *Stewardship*, "There is pride in leadership; it evokes images of direction. There is humility in stewardship; it evokes images of service. Service is central to the idea of stewardship."

As leaders, when we move from control to service, we acknowledge that we are not the central origin of achievement. This shift is an emotional and spiritual breakthrough. Several years ago, I had the privilege of speaking at a Greenleaf Servant Leadership Conference, where Dee Hock also was a keynote speaker. As you may know, Dee Hock, Founder and Chairman of Visa and author of *Birth of the Chaordic Age,* was named one of the eight people who most changed the world through business in the last 50 years. Including himself in a reflection about leadership, Dee said, "When we as leaders get in the bad habit of thinking that other people are there to support our success, we're actually not leaders, we're tyrants. Only until we go through the emotional, psychological, and spiritual transformation to realize our role is to serve others, do we deserve to be called a leader." This is a powerful reframing of the way we typically perceive leadership, isn't it? As we advance through leadership roles, it is easy to get caught up in the "bad habit" of thinking that others are there principally to serve our needs. But once we are conscious of this more powerful perspective, it is easier to move from leadership that is self-serving and short-term to leadership that is constituency-serving and sustainable. In Winston Churchill's often-quoted words, "We make a living by what we get. We make a life by what we give." We are measured as a manager by what we produce. We are judged as a leader by what we give. Or as Einstein said, "It is high time the ideal of success should be replaced with the ideal of service."

Life flows through us, and we simply play our role. Our real job is to serve all the constituencies in our life and, in the process, to appreciate genuinely the fact that only through our interdependence with others do we create value. The more we serve and appreciate others, the more we cooperatively generate value-added contribution. As leaders, if we live for ourselves, we will have only ourselves for support. If we live for our organization, we will

*Effective leaders put words to the formless longings and deeply felt needs of others.*
— Warren Bennis

have people for support. If we live for the world, the whole universe will support us. Serve with purpose and you will marshal far-reaching resources.

A friend of mine had been seeking an opportunity to teach her son about the value of service and giving. The opportunity presented itself after the young boy's birthday party as he prepared to devour one of his gifts: a multilayered box of chocolates. Approaching her son, my friend asked, "Are you happy with this gift?" Wild-eyed, he immediately responded, "Oh, yes!" My friend probed, "What would make you even happier?" Her son had no idea what could possibly add to his joy. His mother then said, "If you gave someone else a chocolate, they would be as happy as you are, and you could feel even happier." The young boy hesitated for a minute. Then, he said, "Let's go see grandma at the nursing home." Off they went to the nursing home. When the child saw the joy on his grandmother's face and felt how it multiplied his joy, he was hooked. Before he left the nursing home, the entire box was gone, and the boy had learned the power and joy of service.

Practice serving authentically. Start by appreciating that there are forces beyond you guiding the whole process. Understand that you are fortunate to have this particular role. Appreciate it; then let your talents and gifts come forth. Bryant Hinckley summed it up well in *Hours with Our Leaders:*

> Service is the virtue that distinguished the great of all times and which they will be remembered by. It places a mark of nobility upon its disciples. It is the dividing line which separates the two great groups of the world—those who help and those who hinder, those who lift and those who lean, those who contribute and those who only consume. How much better it is to give than to receive. Service in any form is comely and beautiful. To give encouragement, to impart sympathy, to show interest, to banish fear, to build self-confidence and awaken hope in the hearts of others, in short—to love them and to show it—is to render the most precious service.

# LEADERSHIP GROWTH PLAN

## INTERPERSONAL MASTERY

Reflect on the learnings that have surfaced as you read this chapter. Consider some new areas of Awareness, Commitment, and Practice, as well as potential obstacles, resources, and signs or measures of success. Reflect on the question, "How could I serve and connect more as a leader?"

1. Areas for Building Awareness:

- _____
- _____
- _____

2. New Commitments to Make:

- _____
- _____
- _____

3. New Practices to Begin:

- _____
- _____
- _____

4. Potential Obstacles:

- _____
- _____
- _____

5. Timeline and Measures of Success:

- _____
- _____
- _____

# CHAPTER FOUR

# CHANGE MASTERY

## *Leading with Agility*

The north shore of Lake Superior is really an awesome sight. The lake is an inland sea unlike any other—the largest body of fresh water in the world. Cool, fresh pine scents the air. Black, rocky cliffs form an imposing backdrop as they disappear into the water's edge. Waterfalls tumble down rivers rushing to their destinations. As calming and refreshing as Superior is, she also is dangerously unpredictable. At a moment's notice, her calm temperament can become a raging force, swallowing huge ships whenever she pleases. Remember Gordon Lightfoot's song about the *Edmund Fitzgerald*? The *Edmund Fitzgerald* was one of her victims.

Growing up in Minnesota, at a young age I received serious warnings about the Great Lake from my elders: "You can only survive the cold water of Superior for four or five minutes." In the spirit of adventure (some might say the spirit of foolishness), I decided to swim the lake.

Donning my wet suit (I'm not completely crazy), I entered the water. As I dove in, the cold water overwhelmed me. It felt breathtakingly, bone-achingly cold. In the first couple of minutes, I believed all the advice of my upbringing. I was sure I could not handle the cold. Then the water in my wet suit started to warm up and everything changed. I became intensely aware of being the only human in this huge watery mass. As I swam near the shore, I closely watched the spears of light passing through the gentle waves. When I swam further into its depth, the blackness of unbelievably deep drop-offs appeared and revealed the lake's immensity. After a short distance, new underwater cliffs and rock formations came into view. Swimming from point to point, I met with an odd mix of feelings. Ecstatic one moment and fearful the next, I sensed that all my emotions were possible and heightened as I explored during this first-time experience.

The cold water kept my heart rate so slow I could go on and on without difficulty. As I progressed, I had the distinct sensation that the lake was choosing to be cooperative with me. Yet, I was aware of the tentativeness of the welcome. If she tired of my adventure, I would be history. I was immersed in the body of the lake, and she was accepting my presence, for the moment. After about three quarters of a mile down the coast, I decided not to overstay my welcome, and I turned back. As I feared, the lake grew impatient. Her waves, which moments ago swelled gently, now rolled harshly and threateningly. Because of the steep cliffs along the shoreline, there was no exit. An enjoyable swim was becoming a dangerous dilemma. All I could do was stay relaxed, tolerate the turbulent, changing waters, and keep my destination in sight. Fortunately, I reached the shore minutes before the lake decided to "wake up." Exhilarated and thankful, I walked up the cliffs. Passing an old-timer along the way, I noticed him staring at me in disbelief. Irritated, he snarled, "You know, a fella could get killed doing that!" He looked astonished as I responded, "I know. But isn't life wonderful?"

> *We all live in suspense, from day to day, from hour to hour; in other words, we are the hero of our own story.*
> — Mary McCarthy

## UNCOVERING THE LEARNING AND GROWTH CONTAINED IN CHANGE

Our lives are much like swimming in Superior. We dive into the water, and we never really know what is going to happen next. We operate under the illusion that life remains constant, but in reality everything is always changing. From breath to breath, we exchange so many atoms we change the makeup of our physiology in a moment. In the course of one year, 98 percent of all our atoms are exchanged for new ones; we are literally new people each year. Our lives are an endless flow of change.

Although it may be true that we can't "step into the same river twice," as Heraclitis once said, once we step in, we are part of that river's flow. Since birth, we have been swept up in a raging, constantly changing, never-ending flow of experience. Some people love the flow of life; others hate it and resist it. But because the flow of the river is a constant, we have no choice in the matter. We have to change. It is part of the price of admission to life. Every moment our atoms are changing; our thoughts are changing; our emotions are changing; our relationships, our marketplace, our finances—change is endless and constant.

> *Changes [in life] are not only possible and predictable, but to deny them is to be an accomplice to one's own unnecessary vegetation.*
> — Gail Sheehy

We have no choice in the matter except for one aspect—mastering our ability to *adapt and to learn.*

Ken Brousseau of Decision Dynamics, an affiliate of Korn/Ferry International, pointed out to me, research shows that as we go up the executive ladder, we need to become increasingly comfortable with uncertainty and sudden change. As leaders, we have to have the "integrative ability" to weave together and make sense of apparently disjointed pieces, crafting novel and innovative solutions. At the same time, we need to have the self- confidence to make decisions on the spot, even in the absence of compelling, complete data. The qualities needed at the top—openness, authentic listening, adaptability—also indicate that leaders need to be comfortable with and able to embrace the "grayness" that comes from other people's ideas. In other words, we have to master our adaptability mentally, emotionally, strategically, and impersonally. Dr. Daniel Vasella, Chairman and CEO of Novartis, who was named "the most influential European business leader of the last 25 years" in a poll of *Financial Times* readers and included in *Time* magazine's 100 most influential people in the world, told the class of 2005 graduates at Mumbai's Indian School of Business, "Be comfortable with seemingly contradictory situations, feelings, and actions. You will of course encounter many people who cannot deal with ambiguity, people who always want simplicity and clarity. So, you as leaders will have to create the clear direction for them."

Based on a study by the Center for Creative Leadership (CCL), the number one issue facing senior leadership today is "Dealing with Complex Challenges." Similar to the Lominger International finding that the number one most important competency in shortest supply today is "Dealing with Ambiguity," the CCL defines complex challenges as problems that:

- Lack a clearly defined solution;
- Remain beyond an individual's or single group's ability to overcome;
- Have significant strategic, cultural, environmental, and marketplace impact;
- Create a paradox of reflection and action;
- Render traditional solutions ineffective;
- Demand flexibility and agility as challenges shift seemingly overnight.

Five leadership skills are required to navigate complex challenges:

- Collaboration rather than heroics;
- Building and mending relationships;
- Participative management;
- Change management and adaptability;
- Risk taking.

Learning to be open to the potential learning contained in all change is no small task. Quite often we are dragged "kicking and screaming" to every lesson. As my colleague Janet Feldman likes to say, "People change more often because they *feel the heat* than because they *see the light.*"

Glenn, a senior executive in a fast-growth, medium-size company, was about to feel the heat. He was extremely bright, with a Ph.D. in a technical discipline. His intellectual prowess was exceptional, but his emotional-interpersonal skills were not as highly developed. As he advanced through the growing organization, these liabilities became more prominent. Unfortunately, Glenn never really comprehended the importance of developing these inner resources. Despite honest feedback, professional assessment, and coaching, he just wasn't ready to grow. Because he didn't see the light, the heat overcame him, and he was terminated.

*Things do not change; we change.*
— Henry David Thoreau

Glenn had never "failed" at anything in his life; the shock of this change was dramatic. For the first time, he was truly vulnerable. As William Bridges would have described it in his insightful writing on change, *Transitions,* Glenn was "between the ending and the new beginning"—he was in the "journey through the wilderness." Fortunately, Glenn took full advantage of personal exploration through his creativity "wilderness." He was finally ready to listen to coaching regarding his style and personality. For the first time, he committed to an action plan to transform his leadership approaches. Within months, he purchased his own business and created a new life. He succeeded because he was open to the purposeful learning contained in the change process. Navigating change is guided by the "true north" of self-discovery.

Learning Agility is a key to unlocking our change proficiency. In fact, research studies by the Center for Creative Leadership, Mike Lombardo of Lominger, Robert Sternberg and his colleagues at Yale University, and Daniel Goleman all point to Learning Agility as being more predictive of long-term potential than raw IQ. Learning Agility is a complex set of skills that allows us to learn something in one situation, situation A, and apply it in a completely different situation, situation B. It is about gathering patterns from one context and then using those patterns in a completely new context so that we can make sense and success out of something we have never seen or done before. In short, Learning Agility is *Change Mastery—the ability to learn, adapt, and apply ourselves in constantly changing conditions.*

With Lominger International's assessment tool *Choices®*, it is possible to measure Learning Agility across four dimensions: Mental Agility, People Agility, Results Agility, and Change Agility. Most executives measured do fine with Mental and Results Agility. Typically, the strongest areas in need of development are People Agility and Change Agility. The core skill need for People Agility? Listening. The core development need in Change Agility? Bringing clarity to ambiguity. As Bob Eichenger, Co-Founder of Lominger International, puts it, "There are 'just' two problems left to solve in business: PEOPLE and CHANGE!!"

Jim was a tough, crusty executive from the "old school." He was extremely bright and got exceptional results, but he also "bored holes" right through people in his drive for excellence. If someone didn't meet his expectations, he would rant and rave. Fewer and fewer people wanted to work with him. His lack of People and Change Agility was starting to limit his career progression. When he was referred to us for executive coaching, I wasn't hopeful. I knew his reputation and doubted he was open to learn or change. After several sessions at our *Executive to Leader Institute*, he was rapidly peeling away layers of self-understanding. To my surprise, he was eagerly open to growth. He didn't intend to impact people negatively. He just didn't know how to get results differently. Years of parental modeling combined with a history of patterning himself after an extremely demanding, insecure boss had set his conditioning in place. Underneath the surface was a caring, sensitive, character-driven person. His family life and personal life were clear evidence of his inner being. Once he found congruence between his inner life and outer life, he evolved as a leader.

## BREAKING OLD PATTERNS AND OPENING UP TO CHANGE

Positive change requires letting go of old patterns and taking a fresh approach. It demands going beyond our preconceived ideas. A story about the relationship of a teacher and student illustrates this principle. A student who thought he had it "all figured out" would visit his teacher each day for personal lessons about life. Despite the teacher's attempts to share her life experience, the student always resisted. One day the teacher took a different approach. When he arrived, the teacher asked the student if he would like some tea. The teacher then proceeded to set the tea table and brought in a huge pot of piping hot tea. She not only filled the student's cup, but once the cup was full, she continued to pour. Tea overflowed. Covering the table and streaming onto the beautiful carpet, the hot tea ruined everything. The student was shocked. He jumped up from his chair and started screaming at the teacher, "Stop! You must be crazy! You're ruining everything! Can't you see what you are doing?" The teacher continued her pouring as if the student wasn't present until the entire pitcher was empty. Only then did she look calmly at the student and respond, "If you want to receive *my* tea, you must keep *your* cup empty."

Like a wise student, we can gain insight only if we are open to change. How often have you taken a detour in traffic and discovered a new, better route? Perhaps you have lost a job or re-lationship, only to connect with a better situation later? How many times has your once-favorite restaurant closed and you discovered a wonderful, new restaurant to replace it? How many difficult or unpleasant experiences end up be-ing the most instructive? Change is always our teacher, pointing new directions, suggesting new options, testing our potentialities. *Change challenges our current reality by forcing a new reality to rush in.* If we're open to it, if our cup is empty, new possibilities flow into our lives. If we're not open to change, we respond to it like an enemy we have to fend off.

> *Change is the timeless interplay of the forces of creation and destruction.*
> — Janet Feldman

Unfortunately, resistance is a losing battle, because change is a relentless opponent. When we resist change, what is the hidden dynamic? We are usually attempting to defend ourselves from the fear of loss. We fear that we will not survive the change without something familiar being lost. This is a truly accurate perception. We will lose something. However, we also are going to gain something. It may be something better, if we are open to the purposeful learning present.

One of the most lucid descriptions of how the change process feels comes from Danaan Parry in *Warriors of the Heart:*

> Sometimes I feel that my life is a series of trapeze swings. I'm either hanging on to a trapeze bar swinging along or, for a few moments in my life, I'm hurtling across space in between trapeze bars.

> Most of the time, I spend my life hanging on for dear life to my trapeze-bar-of-the-moment. It carries me along at a certain steady rate of swing, and I have the feeling that I'm in control of my life. I know most of the right questions and even some of the right answers. But once in a while, as I'm merrily (or not-so-merrily) swinging along, I look out ahead of me into the distance, and what do I see? I see another trapeze bar swing towards me. It's empty, and I know, in that place in me that

knows, that this new trapeze bar has my name on it. It is my next step, my growth, my aliveness coming to get me. In my heart-of-hearts, I know that for me to grow, I must release my grip on this present, well-known bar to move to the new one.

Every time it happens to me, I hope that I won't have to grab the new bar. But in my knowing place I know that I must totally release my grasp on my old bar, and for some moment in time, I must hurdle across space before I can grab onto the new bar. Each time I am filled with terror. It doesn't matter that in all my previous hurdles across the void of unknowing, I have always made it. Each time I am afraid that I will miss, that I will be crushed on unseen rocks in the bottomless chasm between the bars. But I do it anyway. Perhaps this is the essence of what the mystics call the faith experience. No guarantees, no net, no insurance policies, but you do it anyway because somehow, to keep hanging on to that old bar is no longer on the list of alternatives. And so for an eternity that can last a microsecond or a thousand lifetimes, I soar across the dark void of "the past is gone; the future is not yet here." It's called transition. I have come to believe that is the only place that real change occurs. I mean real change, not the pseudo-change that only lasts until the next time my old buttons get punched.

So, if change is so great, why do we fear it? We fear it because change always involves both creation and destruction. As something new is created, something old is destroyed. The bud is destroyed as the flower blooms. The caterpillar is destroyed as the butterfly ascends. Our inhibition comes as we face the prospect of replacing the familiar with the unknown. An existing product fails, and a new one is conceived. A job is lost and a new career begins. At the junction of those two realities, most of us retreat. Usually, it is only after change is thrust upon us that we accept it because we often realize our lives will actually be better.

## DEVELOPING PRESENT-MOMENT AWARENESS TO DEAL WITH CHANGE EFFECTIVELY

Even though the only "place" we can handle change is in the present, most of us live our lives in the past or the future. Until we learn to live our lives in the flow of the present, we can never really deal with change effectively. At the most fundamental level of our lives, there is only the present moment. When we worry about keeping things like they were in the past and avoiding some new, unknown future, we limit our ability to impact our success in the present. If our awareness is cluttered by the "static" of the past and future, we can never focus deeply on the now. As a result, we can never perform to the height of our abilities, particularly in the midst of dynamic change. We need to become now-focused like a professional athlete with single-minded devotion to a task in the midst of very dynamic circumstances. As we build our focus in the present, we begin to gain confidence that we can handle the endless chain of present moments throughout our lives. Change Mastery is about developing an unshakable inner confidence that we can handle and can learn from whatever comes our way. It's an inner confidence that we can deal with real change—unexpected change—not just the run-of-the-mill type of anticipated change. In *Head, Heart and Guts: How the World's Best Companies Develop Leaders*, David Dotlich, Peter Cairo, and Stephen Rhinesmith quote Bill Weldon, Chairman and CEO of Johnson & Johnson: "Sometimes a leader must be able to endure chaos and appreciate it in order to discover the right thing to do."

> *In order to be utterly happy, the only thing necessary is to refrain from comparing this moment with other moments in the past, which I often did not fully enjoy because I was comparing them with other moments of the future.*
> — André Gide

Learning to cultivate this centered, present-moment awareness takes practice on a day-to-day level. We can begin with mundane levels of change and then build our change capacity to higher, more dynamic levels much like an athlete in training. Several months ago, I was returning from a conference in New York City. Like most conferences, it was a combination of some learning, some inspiration, some good speakers, some bad speakers, not enough sleep, and some lousy food. Needless to say, I was ready to return home. My flight back to Minneapolis went smoothly. I arrived at the gate 15 minutes early, my baggage was the first off the plane, and everything went like clockwork. I had "found time" on my hands. My colleague and I had agreed that she would pick me up at the airport after her appointment at a corporate client's offices nearby. We would have lunch and catch up with each other and the business. So I went to the curb and waited. What was I going to do with so much found time in my life—a luxury I rarely experience?

> *Experience is not what happens to a man; it is what a man does with what happens to him.*
> — Aldous Huxley

As I waited near the passenger pickup I could still feel the buzz of New York City in my head, and I could sense the same type of on-edge energy around me. Every person waiting to be picked up seemed to be in an irritable mood. One guy repeatedly pounded his fist on the trunk of an arriving car so his spouse would open the trunk latch. Another, with his cell phone plastered to his cheek, hurled his bags into the back seat and began shouting orders at his companion. As I was observing the scene I said to myself, "This is no way to live. I'm going to make sure my colleague feels appreciated when she gets here. I'm going to wait patiently."

Maintaining this attitude was fairly easy for the first half hour; after all, I had arrived early and had gained a half hour in my life. But when the second half hour began, I was starting to feel those primordial "time is of the essence" rumblings. Catching myself regressing toward the early stages of behavioral evolution demonstrated by my "curb mates," I affirmed, "I don't care if it takes an hour, I'm going to be kind, and in the meantime I'm going to extract whatever learning I can from the present moment." As an entrepreneur and strategist, I frequently live my life in the future. I am thinking of the next new product we'll design, the next presentation I'll make, or the next client I'll meet. At that moment, I truly became aware of what it was like to be in the present. My commitment was so complete, it changed my perception of the entire situation. Letting go of my rigid time focus and my tendency to focus always on the future, I started to notice new things in the present. The air was fresh, crisp, clear. I started to notice how excited the children and dogs in the approaching cars were as they came to pick up moms, dads, grandmas and grandpas, aunts and uncles. Even though the people they were picking up were sometimes grumpy, it didn't matter to the kids or animals—they were in the joy of the present. I started to feel good; I started to unwind and relax. I was dealing with change on an everyday level.

Eventually my colleague phoned. Her client meeting had run slightly longer, midday traffic was a bit snarly, and she regretted the delay. When she did arrive, in keeping with my commitment, I approached her car smiling and buoyant, gave her a warm greeting, and said "Thanks" before she had the chance to apologize for running late. As we headed to a nearby restaurant for lunch, she asked me how the flight was. I said with all sincerity, "The flight was fine, but the last hour of waiting was really terrific. I got some great insights about being present." Her eyes widened as she glanced quickly away from merging traffic and with her sharp tongue-in-cheek wit said, "We need to get you back to the office. You've been away too long!"

How often does our inability to master these everyday situations cause unnecessary stress, tension, loss of productivity, and ineffective relationships? The ability to cope with large and small changes not only improves the quality of our lives, it greatly enhances our effectiveness.

## BRIDGING THE PARADOX OF IMMEDIATE FOCUS AND BROAD AWARENESS FOR LEADING DURING TURBULENT TIMES

*Trust is our trail guide through the wilderness of change.*

— Bill McCarthy

The most effective people I've coached over the years have been able to straddle an important paradox. They not only could sustain a sharp, localized focus in the present moment but at the same time could maintain a broad, visionary context. Being able to maintain a sharp focus and broad comprehension simultaneously is one of the most important qualities for both leadership effectiveness and dealing with change. It reminds me of how I felt in Lake Superior as the waves were kicking up. In order to cope, I had to relax and focus on the quality of my swim stroke while at the same time I kept the goal clearly in mind. Too much attention on one or the other, and the results could have been disastrous. Effective people can bridge these two realities as they navigate through change. Admittedly, doing so can be a real challenge when dramatic, unexpected change brings us to our knees.

Walter was a highly successful human resource executive for a global financial service company. His career had been a steady progression through the organization. He wasn't flashy. He was solid, reliable, responsible, and he got results. He had been loyal to the organization and was totally dedicated to it. When the organizational dynamics rapidly shifted, he didn't fit anymore; he was totally shocked and devastated. Walter conducted a long, tough job search, which took its toll on him and his finances. Eventually he found a new job and sat down with me to celebrate. To my surprise, he couldn't say a word; all he could do was sob deeply and gasp for air. I knew he was happy, but this was extreme. Once composed he said, "Kevin, I probably should have told you this before, but I was so ashamed. I almost took my life two months ago. I went into my garage, sealed off all the doors and cracks, and turned on my car. As I sat there intending to end it all, I remembered your advice—focus on what's important to you and where you want to end up, no matter how difficult things seem. I thought of my daughter and everything I still wanted to do with my life. I flew out of the car and got into the fresh air just in time. I'm so emotional today because I know I didn't just get a job; I got my life."

I am always inspired by these reminders of how our purpose, values, and loved ones are the rudders that help us to navigate through the raging whitewater of change.

## LEARNING TO TRUST OURSELVES AMID DYNAMIC CHANGE

Sometimes even our purpose and values aren't enough to get us through change. At times things are moving so rapidly, all we can do is trust. Some years ago, I was driving about 50 miles per hour in a rainstorm on an interstate highway. As I drove through this blinding rain, I was listening to an audiotape about trusting yourself during times of change. Little did I know how relevant the tape was going to be. A moment later, I heard something hit my roof and realized my fancy, long windshield wiper—my one and only wiper blade—on my fancy new car had flown right over the top of my vehicle. I couldn't see a thing. Naturally, at first I started to panic; then I heard this reassuring voice on the tape encouraging me to trust myself. So I did. I trusted my intuition and navigated my way off the freeway. I'm still amazed that I didn't crash. When I got back to the office, I told a colleague about what had happened and my amazing "trust experience." She advised, "Trust me and get rid of that stupid car!" In times of rapid change, trusting ourselves and our intuition may be our only guide. If that doesn't work, at least buy a car with two wiper blades.

In the business world, maintaining trust through the tough times can be very challenging—particularly when coming face-to-face with failure. At the Toro Company, trust is the bridge to a "freedom-to-fail" environment. Rather than shooting down the teams whose ideas don't work, Toro trusts its people enough to celebrate the "failures." Ken Melrose, former CEO of Toro, shared with me a real-life story of a Toro team that failed in its attempt to save the company time and money by making a new metal hood for a riding lawn mower. Unfortunately, after considerable investment, the project failed. A short time later, Ken called the team to his office. As they gathered outside, they feared the worst. However, when they entered Ken's office, they were completely surprised to be greeted by a celebration with balloons and refreshments. Ken shared with them, "Most innovative ideas don't work out. We need to keep trusting, creating, risking, and celebrating the good 'tries'—particularly when things don't work out." Rooted in the CEO's authentic embodiment of trust and Change Mastery, this "Go for it" attitude spread throughout the company, infusing everyone with energy, confidence, and the genuine permission to innovate.

## LEADERSHIP DEVELOPMENT AS MEASURED BY OUR ABILITY TO ADAPT

Adaptability may be the most crucial quality for effectively dealing with change. I'm sure it's not an exaggeration to say that our personal and professional effectiveness is in direct proportion to our ability to adapt to change. Even the evolution of our species can be measured by its resilient ability to adapt. In *The Guardian,* Buckminster Fuller wrote, "Everyone is too specialized now. We couldn't be getting ourselves into worse trouble since we know that biological species become extinct because they over-specialize and fail to adapt. Society is all tied up with specialization. If nature had wanted you to be a specialist, she'd have had you born with one eye and with a microscope attached to it."

> *Man never made any material as resilient as the human spirit.*
> — Ben Williams

Many people live like they are observing life through the fixed gaze of a microscope. The most fatal obstacle to an effective life is a fixed, unyielding point of view. If we view life in a single-dimensional manner, we will always be disappointed and frustrated. With such a rigid, fixed view, life will never "live up" to our limited definitions. Our lives will be shattered at the first unexpected experience. Since life is growth and motion, a fixed, inflexible view is our greatest threat to an effective life. As Arnold Toynbee said in *Cities on the Move,* "The quality in human nature on which we must pin our hopes is its proven adaptability." If we hope to be more effective leaders, we must pin our hopes on our ability to deal with all life throws at us by changing, adapting, and growing.

> *A change in heart is the essence of all other change and it is brought about by the re-education of the mind.*
> — E. Pethic-Lawrence

## DEVELOPING THE RESILIENCE TO THRIVE IN CHANGE

Change is usually seen as something happening "out there": The world changes, products change, competition changes, systems and processes change, technology changes. While I was coaching a CEO on a major change initiative, he hesitantly said to me, "Let me get this straight: You mean to say that *I'm going to have to change?" All significant change begins with self-change.* As Peter Block writes in *Stewardship,* "If there is no transformation inside each of us, all the structural change in the world will have no impact on our institution."

Moving our concept of change from an outside-in paradigm to an inside-out paradigm has profound implications. When viewed from this perspective, we see change as an internal dynamic—an internal process of learning and development. Change is perceived as something to be mastered from within vs. something only going on outside of us. Ultimately, people resist, adapt, or learn from it. In this regard, all change fundamentally takes place within the person. In his book *Servant Leadership*, Robert Greenleaf expresses it like this: "To the servant leader, the process of change starts in here, in the servant, not out there."

David Prosser, Chairman of RTW, shared with me how he went through the change process, and "reinvented himself":

> Twelve years ago, I was 60 years old, and by all external measures I was very successful. I was standing outside my lake home in suburban Minneapolis, and I happened to notice my huge home with my expensive Mercedes parked in front. In a moment, it dawned on me that despite all this external stuff and success, I wasn't happy. I knew then and there that I needed to transform myself to transform my life. Over the next few years, I committed myself to personal growth.
>
> My personal work culminated in the realization that I wanted to serve people by making a difference in the world. This reinvention of myself eventually led me to found RTW, which is committed to transforming the Workers Compensation system in the United States. If you want to change the world, start by changing yourself—then go out and change the world.

Terry Neil wrote, "Change is a door that can only be opened from the inside." Yet, I know many leaders who, despite enormous competencies and skills, do not make the connection between their own growth and transformation and that of their organization. Transformation is not an event but an ongoing process of knowing who we are, maintaining a clear vision of what we want to create, and then going for it. The same holds true for organizations. All real fundamental development and change begins with self-change.

## CHANGE INITIATIVES RARELY SUCCEED

Most research on personal or organizational change is not pretty. Indeed, most initiatives—between 50 and 75 percent—do not succeed. Just look at these arguments for failure. AT Kearney found 58 percent of all mergers fail to reach their goals and 77 percent added no value. Vantage Partners found that 70 percent of all strategic alliances fail, and Arthur

D. Little found that 67 percent of the *Fortune 500* quality initiatives yielded no significant quality improvements. According to the Hoover Institute, 66 percent of venture capital start-ups failed to return the original investment.

The picture doesn't get any brighter on the individual level, where research shows that 50–75 percent of smoking cessation or weight-loss programs don't succeed either. The conclusion? Change is tough. The critical follow-up question: Why do more than 25 percent work?

As we have seen, Learning Agility is a core factor. In addition, the underlying architecture of agility—our neurophysiology—is fundamental. David Rock, management consultant and author of *Quiet Leadership: Six Steps to Transforming Performance at Work*, and Jeffrey Schwartz, research scientist and author (with Sharon Begley) of *The Mind and Brain*, co-authored an article, "The Neuroscience of Leadership," published in *Strategy+Business* magazine. The article sharply connects the latest research on the brain with leadership imperatives, especially effecting successful change initiatives. In fact, Rock and Schwartz go so far as to tell us, "Managers who understand the recent breakthroughs in cognitive science can lead and influence mindful change: organizational transformation that takes into account the physiological nature of the brain, and the ways in which it predisposes people to resist some forms of leadership and accept others." The authors identify three reasons change initiatives fail:

> *When nothing is sure, everything is possible.*
> — Margaret Drabble

1. Change resistance is real; it makes people physiologically uncomfortable and "amplifies stress";
2. Typical, outside-in behavioristic models don't work for the long term because they rely on external rather than internal drivers;
3. Trying to persuade people to embrace change through outside-in communication initiatives or presentations is not compelling and engaging enough for people.

Based on neuroscience, the authors identify four key elements for successful change:

1. Focus people's attention on the new idea and help them to map a clear vision of what their world will look like from the inside-out;
2. Create an environment in which talking about and sharing this vision is part of the everyday experience;

3. Give people space for reflection and insight to digest the change possibilities from the inside-out;

4. Keep reminding people what is important; leave problems in the past and focus on identifying and creating new behaviors and solutions.

If you lead change in this manner, moving from outside-in approaches to inside-out ones, the "brain of leadership" will keep intrinsically engaged with vision, possibilities, and solutions.

Rock and Schwartz maintain, as do other scientists, including Jon Kabat-Zinn, research scientist and creator of *Mindfulness-Based Stress Reduction (MBSR)*, and Richard Davidson, a neuroscientist at the University of Wisconsin who is studying the influence of meditation on the brain's ability to focus attention, that the more we focus our attention on one thing, we physically change our brain. This means that as leaders we can increase—physiologically—our adaptability to change, and as a result stay more open and engaged as we navigate the change that we want to bring about.

Through 30 years of helping leaders, teams, and organizations to navigate change, we have codified Seven Change Mastery Shifts that can increase our chances of success:

## SEVEN CHANGE MASTERY SHIFTS

- *Change Mastery Shift 1:* From Problem Focus to Opportunity Focus.
  Effective leaders tend to perceive and to innovate on the opportunities inherent in change.
- *Change Mastery Shift 2:* From Short-Term Focus to Long-Term Focus.
  Effective leaders don't lose sight of their long-term vision in the midst of change.
- *Change Mastery Shift 3:* From Circumstance Focus to Purpose Focus.
  Effective leaders maintain a clear sense of purpose, value, and meaning to rise above immediate circumstances.
- *Change Mastery Shift 4:* From Control Focus to Agility Focus.
  Effective leaders understand that control is a management principle that yields a certain degree of results. However, agility, flexibility, and innovation are leadership principles that sustain results over the long haul.
- *Change Mastery Shift 5:* From Self-Focus to Service.
  Effective leaders buffer their teams and organizations from the stress of change by managing, neutralizing, and/or transcending their own stress.

- ***Change Mastery Shift 6:*** From Expertise Focus to Listening Focus.
  Effective leaders stay open and practice authentic listening to stay connected with others and to consider multiple, innovative solutions.

- ***Change Mastery Shift 7:*** From Doubt Focus to Trust Focus.
  Effective leaders are more secure in themselves; they possess a sense that they can handle whatever may come their way; their self-awareness and self-trust are bigger than the circumstances of change.

# REFLECTION

## DEALING WITH CHANGE

Let's take some time to bring all this closer to home. Use the following questions to reflect on how you deal with change in your life:

1. Think about the times you faced major crises or challenges. What qualities or potentialities arose? What qualities would you like to develop further during those times of crisis? What were the key things you learned during those times?

2. When presented with a new experience, what is your first reaction?

3. How do you react when you have invested significant work and effort into something and it doesn't work out? What do you fear most?

4. The next time you face a potential loss, how will you cope differently?

5. Reflect on how well you:

   • Focus on Opportunities vs. Problems

   • Focus on Long Term vs. Short Term

   • Focus on Purpose vs. Circumstance

   • Focus on Adaptability vs. Control

   • Focus on Service vs. Self

   • Focus on Listening vs. Expertise

6. How agile and adaptable are you when it comes to learning from first-time situations?

## MEASURING OUR ABILITY TO DEAL WITH CHANGE

Managing change is a hot topic today. Leaders at all levels of the organization are being challenged to perform like no other time in business history. How well do we prepare our talent to be up to the task? Certainly most of the training in change management and process improvement is valuable. But are we really preparing leaders and all employees to thrive in change? Are we helping people to develop the inner resilience required, or are we throwing them into the lion's den of change and hoping they will somehow survive?

With the rapid change in our information age, the old-world "survival of the fittest" mentality is rapidly becoming obsolete. The whole idea of "fittest" needs to be redefined. No longer a measure of physical prowess or power, it needs to be re-thought in terms of survival of the most aware or survival of the most flexible—mentally, emotionally, and spiritually. The emerging paradigm for success in the coming years will convert from the concept of external exertion to one of internal mastery. Survival of the most aware and most adaptable is becoming the true underlying foundation for lasting effectiveness. Are we gaining mastery from the inside-out to withstand the tumult of change, or are we reacting and defending ourselves against every change that comes our way?

> *Nearly all men can stand adversity, but if you want to test a man's character, give him power.*
> — Abraham Lincoln

If our fear of loss exceeds our personal coping strategies, we will be overwhelmed, and therefore ineffective in dealing with change. It all boils down to accessing the Learning Agility within us. Imagine how bold and wonderful our lives would be if our purpose, vision, and resilience were so strong that fear would not have a hold over us. Outstanding leaders like Franklin Delano Roosevelt understood this dynamic: "We have nothing to fear but fear itself." These words are spoken from a place of true character—a place of unshakable inner conviction, strength, and awareness. They are not merely a cleverly crafted phrase but an expression of a deep, internally driven leader. Imagine your life totally free of fear. You would harbor no financial fear, no fear of failure, no fear of loss—no fear whatsoever. How would you live? How would you change? If you could not fail, what would you do?

## EIGHT POINTS OF AWARENESS FOR LEADING WITH AGILITY

As you develop Change Mastery, keep the following principles in mind:

*1. Be Open to the Learning:* When we resist change, all our energy is bound up in the effort to maintain the status quo. In this restricted state of awareness, we miss the lessons trying to be delivered to us. There's no need to deny the challenges you are experiencing. Encourage yourself to open up consciously to the learning hidden in the changing circumstances. Consider challenging career assignments that go against the grain. Grow with the flow . . . and grow within the creative tension of change.

*2. Practice Present-Moment Awareness:* In the midst of change, we often cope by escaping mentally and emotionally to the past or future. As a result, we rarely live in the present. Imagine a tennis player preoccupied with his past matches or potential future matches in the midst of a dynamic set. Would he or she be successful? Developing focus in the present moment allows us to begin to "connect up" a series of present-moment successes into a lifetime of effectiveness. Think about it: Isn't the present moment our only real shot at success?

*3. Integrate Immediate Focus and Broad Awareness:* It may sound like a paradox, but highly effective people have learned to integrate a localized focus with comprehensive awareness. They zero in on the present moment without losing the broader sense of their vision and purpose. Being deeply focused yet simultaneously aware of the meaningful context of our lives is one of the keys to inside-out success. Many successful people describe their broad, purposeful awareness to be like a screen on which all the focused, localized events of their lives are connected in a meaningful way.

*4. Trust Yourself:* Sometimes the "G-forces" of change are so intense, all we can do is sit back, hold on, and trust that everything will work out. Developing our inner ability to trust is crucial as we hurl through the air between our trapeze bars. As André Gide wrote, "One does not discover new lands without consenting to lose sight of the shore for a very long time." The essence of Change Mastery is self-trust.

*5. Develop Resiliency through Mental-Emotional Stretching:* Our current state of development or personal evolution can be measured directly by our ability to adapt. Our life shrinks and expands in proportion to our personal flexibility. To "limber up," start to stretch yourself in the mundane, everyday events of life. How are you adapting to the slow traffic? How are you reacting to being late for an important presentation or being open to someone else's "unusual" style or background? What is your response to trying something new? Gradually increase your emotional-mental-spiritual flexibility to make yourself more agile for life's major events. Follow the same principles used for physical training: stretch, don't strain—micro-millimeters of daily progress are sufficient. As we regularly practice this type of training, our elasticity may be experienced as a calm and centered sense of self in the midst of unpredictable events. As our agility becomes more advanced, we begin to have an inner sense that we can handle whatever comes our way. Follow the advice of Benjamin Franklin, "Be not disturbed at trifles or at accidents, common or unavoidable."

**6. Remember That All Significant Change Begins with Self-Change:** Recently a CEO of a global organization asked us to both facilitate leadership development for his top people and help them get a deeper, more intimate sense of their high-potential talent. We have a process called *LeaderSuccession^sm* that intimately involves a sponsor, often a CEO or another key executive, and a small group of six to eight people who get to have a deep leadership development experience where they get lots of self-awareness and awareness from colleagues as they learn from the inside-out and the outside-in. When this CEO asked if he should be there to "kick it off," we said, "Absolutely not. You need to be there for the *entire* two and a half days." Although he hesitated, he agreed. The program was a big success. Unfortunately, many succession and talent-review processes just do a superficial review of talent, focusing on assessments and rankings. During this program, the top talent built new self-awareness, learned teaming skills, and understood the powerful balance of personal power and relational power. Also, the CEO really got to know some of his key talent. But . . . the biggest, most unexpected benefit was the CEO's own growth and development. Presumably, he was there to "observe." To his credit, he shifted from observation to participation, and he was the most surprised to find that he accelerated his own progression. Additionally, he modeled the open, developmental behavior he wanted to see in others. *If you want to develop your people, be the development you want to see.* Remember the Change Mastery mantra, "All significant change begins with self-change."

> *We may not transform reality, but we may transform ourselves. And if we transform ourselves, we might just change the world a little bit.*
>
> — Gary Snyder

**7. Practice the Change Mastery Shifts:** To deal with change as a leader, constantly challenge yourself to make the seven Change Mastery Shifts:

- Move from Problem Focus to Opportunity Focus.
- Move from Short-Term Focus to Long-Term Focus.
- Move from Circumstance Focus to Purpose Focus.
- Move from Control Focus to Agility Focus.
- Move from Self Focus to Service Focus.
- Move from Expertise Focus to Listening Focus.
- Move from Doubt Focus to Trust Focus.

Making these shifts will transform your leadership effectiveness by shifting from being coping-driven to being character-driven.

**8. *Take the Leap:*** Accept the fact that you will naturally feel some hesitation and anxiety when facing the trapeze bar. Learning to see beyond the fear of loss and into purpose and vision gives us the courage to take the leap. I like to tell people as they are facing the "trapeze bar" of the moment, "Hey, Buddy, can you dare some change?" When faced with going to "a new edge," think of the bold inner confidence expressed in this Zen poem:

> Ride your horse along the edge of the sword,
> Hide yourself in the middle of the flames,
> Blossoms of the fruit tree bloom in the fire,
> The sun rises in the evening.

# LEADERSHIP GROWTH PLAN

## CHANGE MASTERY

Reflect on the learnings that have surfaced as you read this chapter. Reflect on the question, "How can I enhance my agility and learning during times of challenging change?"

1. Areas for Building Awareness:

   - _____
   - _____
   - _____

2. New Commitments to Make:

   - _____
   - _____
   - _____

3. New Practices to Begin:

   - _____
   - _____
   - _____

4. Potential Obstacles:

   - _____
   - _____
   - _____

5. Timeline and Measures of Success:

   - _____
   - _____
   - _____

CHAPTER FIVE

# RESILIENCE MASTERY
## *Leading with Energy*

In preparing to write this book, I personally interviewed 62 CEOs and presidents of corporations. The purpose of these meetings was to solicit their views regarding our leadership models and to have them challenge our viewpoints. Additionally, we conducted a survey to discover which areas of mastery corporate leaders perceived as most relevant to their leadership effectiveness and which areas they viewed as the most challenging. The results of our interviews were very clear-cut: 75 percent of the CEOs and presidents saw Personal Mastery as the most relevant to their leadership effectiveness, while 67 percent saw Interpersonal Mastery as the second most relevant. However, 92 percent of them selected Resilience Mastery as the most challenging personally.

For most leaders I meet, balancing work and home life still is a lofty, never-achieved goal. Yet, the more I encounter the time-oriented, mechanistic formula of work/life balance (i.e., working a certain number of hours, exercising four times a week, spending a certain number of evenings a week with family), the less useful and relevant I find it. Although each day brings nearly impossible demands on our time, with too many meetings, obligations, and 24/7 connectivity in a global marketplace, it is our resilience and energy that are stressed daily, not the clock. Most days begin like a sprint and then turn into a triathlon of meetings, e-mails, and presentations. Let's face it, "time is a finite resource." We get 24 hours, no matter how we carve it up. However, shifting our focus from *time management* to *energy leadership* can allow us to discover our own unique formula for *sustained energy and resilience* throughout each day. When we are calm and focused, we are more on top of the demands of leadership. Conversely, when our energy is low or manic, everything seems on top of us.

When I met for the first time with Tim, a senior executive in a global industrial products company, I sensed a few cracks in his macho, results-oriented armor. I asked how he was doing, and his quick response was, "Fine, but traveling lots." I asked how many weekends he had been home over the last six months, and he had to stop and think. "Well . . . let me see . . . four . . . or maybe five. It's fine. Really. Just part of the job." Tim's career-fueled denial was getting harder and harder to dismiss. While he was racking up diamonds on his frequent flyer status, Tim was missing countless school and social events. Interestingly, his mind seemed to be handling it, but his body, spirit, and family weren't faring so well. It was cause for great concern because mental acuity can be very misleading, while energy and resilience levels tend to be quite telling.

> *Time is a limited resource; energy is an unlimited Source.*
>
> — Katie Cooney

Ariel, a marketing executive and mother of three children under the age of seven, told me that she handles "normal" days of work and family just fine. The worst thing for her is when she has to be on the phone at night for hours with customers in Asia. She doesn't get enough sleep, and that throws everything else off kilter the next day. She is worn out, more anxious, and "loses it" easily with people at work and with the kids at home.

David, the CFO of a mid-size company and another "extreme" traveler, shared his wake-up call with me. Returning from a two-week business trip, he was lifting his luggage out of the trunk of his car when his six-year-old son walked into the garage from the house. Surprised by the unfamiliar sight of a man in his garage, the child ran back into the house screaming. His son actually mistook him for an intruder! In that moment, David knew it was time to re-enter all parts of his life. The essence of our challenge as leaders: finding enough energy, resilience, and connection to serve all our important life priorities without any one of them, or us, "running out" in a panic.

## CHALLENGES OF RESILIENCE FOR EXECUTIVES

I'm no exception. My life has been a whirlwind since December 2006, when Leader-Source joined Korn/Ferry International. Now further into the integration, we are delighted with all of the synergies and new opportunities we are creating. With 80 offices in 40 countries and more than 200 coaches, we have an unparalleled ability to expand the reach of our talent management programs around the world. Like Tim and David, I'm traveling all over the globe, collecting reward after reward. The demands of my life are definitely challenging my mental, physical, emotional, and spiritual well-being. The sudden changes of this extraordinary period of growth definitely present constant challenges to my own mastery of Resilience. Fortunately, my life experience—learning from previous growth spurts and the foundation of my practices—has helped me to manage my energy through this expansion.

Twelve years ago, I naively thought I had this work/life balance thing pretty well figured out. On some levels I did as long as my life didn't change beyond expectations. However, our leadership development and executive coaching practice took a sudden leap forward, doubling in size over a very short period. With this sudden growth spurt, my life was wonderfully out of balance. I say "wonderfully" because I loved the work. My problem was that it was too much of a good thing. I felt as if I was sitting at an incredible feast, and I was not able to push away from the table. The "indigestion" of too much work was causing harmful symptoms: strain in relationships, reduced energy level, diminished passion, and physical stress. All this culminated in serious health issues. Unfortunately, the intensity of these symptoms had to become painful enough for me to pay attention. I definitely needed to shift my focus from a time-oriented balancing act to an energy and resilience-rich process. It took a few months of focused attention to take my life back. Over time, I was able to lay an even stronger foundation for dealing with future growth challenges, and it has paid off for me during this current one.

Although I feel somewhat more confident in Resilience Mastery now, I would agree with my CEO colleagues that balance or Resilience Mastery is the most difficult of the seven mastery areas. This eloquent, witty insight by E. B. White helps me keep perspective: "I arise in the morning torn between a desire to *save the world* and a desire to *savor the world*. This makes it very hard to plan the day!" How often do you feel the tension between your desire to serve and your need for self-care? It's not always easy to choose because both are important.

## WHAT HAPPENED TO THE LIFE OF LEISURE?

What happened to the life of leisure we were supposed to be living by now? Weren't we supposed to be working 20 to 30-hour weeks with lots of leisure time on our hands? Not too long ago, futurists were predicting this as the natural outcome of our automated, computer age. Very few of us would say that our lives have become more leisurely. The 40-hour week became the 60-hour week, and in a *Fortune,* CNNMoney.com article, November 2005, Jody Miller writes, "The 60-hour weeks once thought to be the path to glory are now practically considered part-time." In the same article, Bill George, former CEO of Medtronic, Inc., says, "It didn't use to be this intense. It got much worse starting 15 years ago, when we went to this 80-hour week." Miller reports that George and others warn, "Top executives are increasingly strung out. . . . Service firms in consulting, law, and

*Managers control resources;
leaders multiply energy.*
— Anne Tessien

investment banking have built 80-hour weeks into their businesses. If it keeps up, the toll could make itself felt not only on companies, but on the nation, eroding productivity growth in an era when global competition has never been more intense."

Increasingly, most people would say life is a raging stream of "have-to-dos" vs. "want-to-dos." Each new "convenience" like cell phones, Blackberries, e-mail, and text-messaging simultaneously delivers some "free time" with ten new things to do. Is it possible that doing more and more is not the answer?

Particularly in career settings, the potential for feeling overwhelmed is great. High-performing people naturally want to achieve more and more. High-performing organizations exhibit an insatiable desire to "pile" more and more responsibility on key people. On top of this, many companies, thinking they need to operate leaner and leaner, require fewer people to carry out more work. At precisely the time when people need to draw on greater resources of energy and drive, the reserves may be depleted. Finding ways to refresh and to revitalize ourselves has never been more crucial to our productivity and satisfaction. Research reported by Tony Schwartz and Catherine McCarthy in the October 2007 *Harvard Business Review* article, "Manage Your Energy, Not Your Time," addresses this issue. "The core problem with working longer hours is that time is a finite resource. Energy is a different story. Defined in physics as the capacity to work, energy comes from four main wellsprings in human beings: the body, emotions, mind and spirit." This is a salient issue for individuals, teams, and the organizations we lead. Schwartz and McCarthy continue, "To effectively reenergize their workforces, organizations need to shift from getting more out of people to investing more in them, so they are motivated—and able—to bring more of themselves to work every day. To recharge themselves, individuals need to recognize the costs of energy-depleting behaviors and then take responsibility for changing them, regardless of the circumstances they're facing." The research Schwartz and McCarthy describe in the *Harvard Business Review* article has gotten attention because it reported the impressive, tangible results of a group of employees called the "pilot energy management group," against the performance of a control group. The study found that "the participants outperformed the controls on a series of financial metrics. . . . They also reported substantial improvements in their customer relationships, their engagement with work, and their personal satisfaction." Resilience and energy fuel results.

## MOVING FROM TIME AND EFFICIENCY TO ENERGY AND RESILIENCE

| TIME MANAGEMENT | VS. | ENERGY LEADERSHIP |
|---|---|---|
| Management Focus | | Leadership Focus |
| Controlling Limited Resources | | Multiplying Energy |
| Goals and Outcomes | | Passion and Purpose |
| Personal/Team/Organizational Productivity | | Personal/Team/Organizational Engagement |
| Trying to Get on Top of Things | | Being on Top of Things |
| Feeling Time-Starved and Disappointed | | Feeling Engaged and Satisfied |

If we are going to shift from managing our time to supporting and managing our energy—the real fuel that helps us get things done, take on difficult challenges, and be present in our relationships—we need to do it in all domains of our lives: physical, mental, emotional, and spiritual. Of course, we also need to have the basic physical energy necessary to perform, which requires physical self-care: the basics of good health, good nutrition, exercise, sleep, and rest that support our productivity. Beyond that is the natural energy derived from engagement in life-affirming, meaningful activities, as opposed to activities that drain our energy and are devoid of meaning.

Have you ever noticed how differently you feel about doing something at the end of the day that you really like and want to do—say, going for a dance lesson, attending a sporting event, working in the garden, or having a quiet dinner with friends—as opposed to something that you really dislike and don't want to do—working on a financial line-item report, attending a committee meeting, cleaning out the garage, or maybe going to a dance lesson? (One person's energy booster can be another person's energy drainer.) Let's stop for a moment and remember how we feel in those situations. When we have to force ourselves to do something, we feel deflated, tired, bored, and anxious to find a way to put it off until the next day, when we will have more energy. But when we are faced with doing something we really enjoy, our energy is abundant.

That energy is the key—the instrument to joy, purpose, resilience, and sustained success. Let's step out on this ledge a little further. What if we had so much of what we wanted in our life, we didn't have time for what we didn't want? Step back for a moment and imagine what that would feel like.

A results-oriented, yet unassuming man, Rick had a long list of achievements. However, Rick had ignored one very important constituent for quite some time: himself and his health. As a new executive in a global firm, he came to our *Executive to Leader Institute* pro-

> *It's not only the scenery you miss by going too fast—you also miss the sense of where you're going and why.*
> — Eddie Cantor

gram with the same determination he brought to all his challenges. We learned that Rick really loved to be outdoors and longed for this rejuvenation. Feedback told us that people around him did not feel connected to him and some lacked trust as a result. They had contact with him only at formal events, and they didn't know him very well. Rick also told us that his doctor recommended that he lose some weight. We challenged Rick to come up with a daily practice that would build energy, health, and relationships all at once. At first, he struggled to come up with something. Then, he came to us with his commitment. He would take daily short walks, and three times weekly he would invite employees and colleagues to join him, for no other reason than to get to know each other. Rick found that he really looked forward to the walks in all seasons. He was energized by them, and this energy was evident to his colleagues that joined him. He returned happier and more energetic. In fact, he felt buoyant. As he increased his energy, he multiplied it with others. Leaders must access and expand energy in every way possible to sustain success.

Unfortunately, many executives minimize the value of resilience to enhance leadership performance. A while ago, I met with a senior executive in a major corporation who was keenly interested in our coaching and development programs. He was extremely engaged by how we integrated the Personal Mastery, Leadership Mastery, Interpersonal Mastery, and Career/Purpose Mastery in our *Executive to Leader Institute*. However, he was totally against including Resilience Mastery as part of his program. He strongly objected to the relevance of it. "What does having a more resilient life have to do with my leadership performance anyway?" Because I knew this person's reputation for blowing up at people for insignificant things, I knew he needed more resilience, and I needed to press the point. However, even after a lengthy discussion on how being more resilient directly affects how we lead, as well as our ability to cope with the endless demands of highly responsible positions, he was still resistant. Rather than press him further, I gave him some materials and suggested we get together in a few days. The meeting never happened. The 42-year-old executive died of a massive heart attack two days later. Incorporating resilience practices into our lifestyle is not a luxury; it is a necessity. As leaders, resilience allows us first to survive and second to thrive.

## WHAT HEALTHY, PRODUCTIVE 100-YEAR-OLDS CAN TEACH LEADERS

A five-year study, completed by Dr. Leonard Poon of the University of Georgia, revealed some interesting principles influencing resilience. In his study of 97 active, productive people over 100 years of age, he found that they had mastered four common characteristics:

1. *Optimism:* They tended to have a positive view of the past and future. They were not dominated by worry or negativity.
2. *Engagement:* They were actively involved in life. They were not passive observers, allowing life to pass them by.
3. *Mobility:* They stayed active physically. One person was an aerobics instructor; most walked or gardened daily.
4. *Adaptability to Loss:* They had an extraordinary ability to stay balanced by adapting to and accepting change and loss. Even though most of them had lost their families and friends, they still had a zest for learning and living.

The study also uncovered one interesting surprise. These 100-year-olds tended to eat whatever they wanted. In fact, most of them had high-fat, high-calorie diets. What was their secret to a healthy lifestyle? They were happy, involved, active, resilient people. They appeared to have mastered the joy of living.

## RESILIENCE IS A DYNAMIC PROCESS

Resilience Mastery is not a static, rigid process; it is a type of centered fluidity that lets us go in any direction with ease and agility. Being resilient means we can recover our balance even in the midst of action. Separating our career, personal, family, emotional, and spiritual lives into distinct pieces and then trying to balance the parts on a scale doesn't work. Managing the entire dynamic is the key. We need to locate the dynamics that run through all the pieces and then influence our resilience at that level. Mastery of Resilience is about practicing inner and outer behaviors that keep us grounded and centered so we can deal with all the dynamics outside. As we build more resilience, we can do more with ease. Actually, when we are resilient, we can shoulder more weight with less effort because we are strong at our very foundation. We have that foundation to handle unforeseen crises instead of the anxiety and constant fear that one more unexpected problem will take us down. Finding ways to build that resilient foundation from the inside-out is the key to Resilience Mastery.

Charlotte was hesitant and fearful about taking on another executive position. She had left her previous company and position because she was completely burned out. Char-

> *Energy and persistence*
> *conquer all things.*
> — Benjamin Franklin

lotte's husband always was and always has been fully supportive of her demanding professional career, and her children, teenagers, needed a different kind of parenting from when they were younger, so Charlotte decided to get back in the game, but not without coaching this time. Charlotte is action-oriented, so it was important to help her find new behaviors that she could implement easily and would yield results quickly. We helped her formulate a plan that addressed the four domains of resiliency: physical, mental, emotional, and spiritual. Since Charlotte carried some extra weight, we suggested a regular routine of weight training, cardiovascular exercise, and conscious food choices, which would help her attain a healthier weight and more physical energy. She noticed an increase in her stamina, even on more sedentary days of meetings, and her stamina increased dramatically when she lost 20 pounds. An important aspect of Charlotte's Resilience Mastery plan was her lake cabin and boat, as well as her orientation toward visual images. Even when Charlotte couldn't actually be at the lake to restore herself, accessible photos and mental images of the lake during the various seasons were extremely helpful to her. Time with family and friends, stretches of quiet time, short breaks for walks, and visualizations and breathing have helped Charlotte re-enter her professional life in a new, more sustaining way.

## TEN SIGNS OF RESILIENCE MASTERY

So what are some of the signs of Resilience Mastery?

- Smooth, abundant energy
- Ability to focus deeply
- Internally driven motivation
- Optimism
- Fulfilling, intimate relationships
- Creativity and innovation
- Vitality and enthusiasm
- Little or no usage of caffeine, nicotine, or alcohol
- Achievement with ease

- Optimal productivity
- Feeling "on top of" situations

## TEN SIGNS OF LACK OF RESILIENCE

What are some of the signs of lack of resilience?

- Nervous, manic energy
- Wandering, unfocused mind
- Externally driven motivation
- Negativity
- Strain in relationships
- Dullness, lack of inspiration
- Depression and fatigue
- Regular usage of caffeine, nicotine, or alcohol
- Achievement via strain and effort
- Less than optimal productivity
- Feeling "overshadowed" by situations

## NATURE'S RESILIENCE: REST AND ACTIVITY

How do we go about finding more resilience in our lives? The best model for resilience exists in nature. All resilience in nature evolves through alternate cycles of rest and activity. The cycles of day and night and the seasonal cycles constantly balance a rest phase with an active phase. Nature expresses its vitality in the active phase. Nature reconnects with its vitality in the rest phase. Each phase interacts in just the right combination to achieve dynamic balance. Our lives are similar with one major difference: We get to choose the quantity and quality of activity, as well as the quantity and quality of rest. When we choose inappropriately, our life is out of whack. When we choose well, we experience vitality. Nature lets us choose freely, but she also gives us immediate feedback on how well we have chosen. As we learn to listen better, our energy and resilience increase.

Jack Groppel and Bob Andelman, authors of the 1999 book *The Corporate Athlete: How to Achieve Maximal Performance in Business Life*, rocked the corporate world when they applied the principles of stress and recovery used coaching world-class athletes to working with corporate leaders, teams, and organizations. In a recent article, "Stress & Recovery:

Important Keys to Engagement," James Loehr and Jack Groppel echo what we see in nature and apply it to the "corporate athlete": "Stress is the stimulus for growth; recovery is when growth occurs. If you have no recovery, you have no growth." To illustrate their point in athletic terms, they describe the four levels of recovery—physical, mental, emotional, and spiritual—that a professional tennis player has to shift into for recovery within seconds between points. The authors assert, "Everything they do can be accomplished by business people." Pressing us further, they suggest asking ourselves the question, "How valuable would it be for my people to learn to recapture energy in small time intervals during their workday?" The result, they say, is "more productivity at work and ample reserves left over for home. As a result performance goes up and loyalty improves."

> *Stress is in the eye of the beholder; it can inspire a purposeful vision or it can cast a dark shadow.*
> — Dina Rauker

Most imbalances in our society come from two major sources: We tend to overdo our activity, and we tend to underdo our rest. The formula for most of us to foster more resilience in our lives usually involves two things:

1. Improve the quality of our activity and reduce the quantity somewhat.
2. Improve the quality and quantity of our rest.

## THE ELEVEN POINTS OF RESILIENCE MASTERY

What are some ways to satisfy both of these requirements? Although there could be many others, I've found Eleven Points of Resilience Mastery that can help center our lives in an integrated, holistic way:

*1. Be on Purpose, but Be Aware:* Of all the points of resilience, discovering our purpose is one of the most important. It is our centered position of strength. When we are on-purpose, it is most difficult for others to knock us off balance. So often, while we are caught up in the activity of our lives, we seldom ask ourselves, "Why?" As Thoreau reflected, "It is not enough to be busy; so are the ants. The question is, what are we busy about?" Rather than simply amassing a great pile of achievements or experiences, our lives can be about burning a passionate fire that illuminates our way. But we have to be careful. As our passionate purpose burns strongly, our devotion to it also can cause us to drain our energy. We become so single-minded about our mission, we can begin to ignore our rest, physical needs, or relationships. We must be purposeful, but not let the passion burn us out.

I'm often asked by people about my ability to meditate daily, write books, and have close relationships while running a consulting business and traveling globally. People conjecture, "How do you do it? You must be so disciplined about your daily schedule." I'm always taken aback. It's never about a disciplined schedule for me; it's about what I want to include in my schedule. I meditate, write, have relationships, run my business, and travel because I love it. If people said to me, "You must really love what you do. You must feel passionate and purposeful about your life," I would probably be a little embarrassed, but at the same time, I would feel at home with their comment. Purpose and passion compel us to achieve multiple goals with greater energy and stamina.

*2. Foster Your Energy vs. Managing Time:* Time management is a function of the clock. It is outside ourselves. It is the domain of management. Energy management is the domain of leadership. It comes from within, has the capacity to increase, to go beyond what is. Therefore, doing everything possible to keep our energy level higher and more abundant than the challenges we face is the key to resilience. When energy is low, life and leadership are a drag. When our energy is strong, we can face tremendous pressure and challenges, and we can thrive despite them. If "the world belongs to the energetic," as Emerson said, then let's find all the practices necessary to enhance our energy levels.

What practices have you abandoned that were your energy boosters? What people in your life generate energy? What people deplete your energy? What fitness, fun or spiritual practices give you the greatest lift? Put together an energy plan. Include only the practices that you really love. These are your sustainable energy enhancers.

*3. Learning to Exercise with Ease:* You may be surprised to hear this from someone who competed in triathlons for years, but we are killing ourselves with our unenlightened approaches to exercise. Unknowingly, most people don't exercise; they punish themselves. Many get so disconnected from their body that they mistakenly associate the fatigue they feel with a "high." The "no pain, no gain" mentality usually creates more fatigue, stress, and risk for injury than any real type of fitness. We really need to re-think exercise.

We need to go to a deeper level and ask ourselves, "What is the *purpose* of exercise?" Certainly losing weight, looking good, or setting a new personal record are some superficial

*Fitness has to be fun. If it is not play, there will be no fitness. Play, you see, is the process. Fitness is merely the product.*

— George Sheehan

purposes, but not the most profound, compelling ones. If you are a professional athlete, the purpose of exercise may be to express your spirit in the physical realm as no one else has done before.

Most of us, however, are not professional athletes, and we need to find a meaning of fitness for us. Isn't that meaning closer to the Greek ideal of mind-body integration? Isn't it about rejuvenating ourselves, bringing more vitality, energy, and joy of movement into our lives? For me, the purpose of exercise is to strengthen our vehicle so it can support more effectively our overall life purpose. It's about being present and in the joy, "enjoying" the movement of body and spirit. A pretty heady framework for push-ups, dumbbells, and sweaty runs, isn't it?

Some of our more driven executive clients proudly tell us they "exercise every day without fail." When we ask them if they enjoy it, they look a bit confused and respond, "Well no, but I do it *every day*, anyway!" If you have to force yourself to run, then find something else that you enjoy doing.

Activities you enjoy bring energy and resilience. Activities you dislike create energy drain and imbalance. The joy of the activity itself is as health-giving as the aerobic effect. Besides, if you don't enjoy it, you will either "succeed" in becoming a more rigid person or you will quit it eventually anyway. What we love, we stay with. Find ways that you love to move your physical being.

The most enlightened perspective I have found on exercise is in the book *Body, Mind & Sport* by Dr. John Douillard. Using ancient techniques of mind-body integration, he guides people through a program to experience the "zone," the exercise high, every time. People start to truly enjoy exercise as they find their minds deeply composed in the midst of dynamic physical activity. Within this new paradigm, Douillard writes, "This gives us a new, uniquely challenging fitness goal. We're no longer content to see how much we can do; we want to know how effortlessly we can do it!" You may want to read Douillard's book to get a complete picture. In the meantime, consider some of these suggestions for more enlightened exercise:

- Find an activity (or activities) you love.
- Set the uncompromising goal that you are going to feel good throughout the exercise

program. If you feel any strain, go more slowly. If you lose your breath or cannot comfortably hold a conversation with a training partner, slow down.

- Breathe in and out *through your nose* the entire workout. If you have to breathe through your mouth, you're straining, so slow down.
- Always warm up by walking or very slowly beginning your activity for 10–15 minutes before you start exercising.
- Do light stretching only after you are warmed up—stretch, never strain. Consider incorporating gentle, effective stretching into your routine.
- Maintain an awareness of your body and how it feels during the entire workout. If you do not feel comfortable throughout the workout, slow down or stop until you do.
- Walk for 5–10 minutes to cool down. Do more light stretching.
- Start gauging your fitness by how good you feel during and after the activity, not by how hard you worked yourself or how far or fast you went.

If you follow this process regularly, you will enjoy the exercise session and remain more balanced. Most athletes are always on the verge of fatigue, illness, and injury, so they are always somewhat imbalanced. Exercise with ease. You will improve your fitness, energy, and quality of life, all in one process.

If you are having trouble finding time to keep active, remember, Thomas Jefferson believed in getting two hours of exercise every day. If someone who wrote the U.S. Declaration of Independence, became president, and was secretary of state could find two hours a day, you can find 20–30 minutes a few times a week! Try two 20-minute walks per day. Use them as your breaks. Clear your mind and get some cardio at the same time. Check with a physician before you begin any exercise program.

*4. Deal with Life-Damaging Habits:* Poor lifestyle choices account for more misery, suffering, death, and imbalance in our society than any other single or multiple cause.

The choice to smoke cigarettes, for instance, is the cause of more than 420,000 deaths each year in the United States alone. That's seven times higher than the number of Americans who died in the entire Vietnam War. The World Health Organization has identified smoking as the number one killer on the planet. This represents only one lifestyle choice! What about the abuse of alcohol and drugs, as well as poor choices in the areas of food, relationships, and exercise? It has been estimated that more than 70 percent of all disease has a basis in poor lifestyle decisions. It may sound dramatic, but lifestyle decisions can lead you in one of two directions—life or death.

It's hard to fathom how much imbalance life-damaging habits cause. Most of us don't engage in behaviors to harm ourselves. The problem is that we have mistaken certain habits for happiness. We unknowingly exchange a short-term fix for long-term damage. How do we retreat from behaviors we know are hurting us? Mark Twain captured the challenge of moving away from certain behaviors when he said, "Habit is habit, and not to be flung out of the window, but coaxed downstairs a step at a time." The steps for coaxing them downstairs are several:

> *Habit is habit, and not to be flung out the window, but coaxed downstairs a step at a time.*
> — Mark Twain

- Admit that the habit is damaging to you and possibly others. Go deeply into all the negative effects this habit is having on you. Until you acknowledge the problem, you won't have any genuine motivation to change.
- Get professional or peer support to help you. It's unlikely you can do it on your own, or you would have done it already.
- Find positive behaviors to replace the old addictions. As the old proverb goes, "You can more easily drive out a tough nail with another nail." Replace smoking with exercise, desserts with fruit, soda with juice, and so forth.
- Continually repeat the first three steps if the habits take hold again or new ones appear.

> *Courage and perseverance have a magical talisman, before which difficulties and obstacles vanish into air.*
> — John Quincy Adams

Habits that involve the overuse of stimulants like coffee and nicotine are particularly indicative of lack of resilience. The need for artificial stimulants typically is masking the deep fatigue within. To help yourself as you ease out of these particular habits, additional rest and meditation greatly accelerate the rebounding process.

*5. Avoid Taking Yourself So Seriously:* Humor and light-heartedness energize mind, body, and spirit. The more rigid and self-centered we are, the more out of balance we become. Proverbs 17:22 captures the essence of this principle: "A cheerful heart is good medicine." Imagine yourself in your most secure, strong moments. Aren't these the times you can laugh at yourself and observe life in a playful manner? Letting go of our own rigid, external mask brings joy and energy into our life. Harriet Rochlin wrote, "Laughter can be more satisfying than honor; more precious than money; more heart-cleansing than prayer."

Daniel Pink, in *A Whole New Mind*, writes about Madan Kataria, a physician in Mumbai, India, who likes to laugh and has started laughter clubs, believing that laughter can be like a "benevolent virus—that can infect individuals, communities, even nations." With the proliferation of laughter clubs, Dr. Kataria hopes to inculcate an epidemic that will "improve our health, increase our profits, and maybe even bring world peace." Pink also writes, "Play is emerging from the shadows of frivolousness and assuming a place in the spotlight. . . . Play is becoming an important part of work, business and personal well-being." Have you ever seen an energetic dog let loose onto an open field—the pure joy and exhilaration of its run, stretching its boundaries, expressing its freedom? It's wonderful to witness. Maybe it's time to set your seriousness aside and take a joyous run into your open field!

Treat life like a play. Be concerned about the plot, your fellow actors, and doing it well. But don't take yourself too seriously. In the broader scheme of things, it's just a role in the cosmic play. Effective leaders have clear perspective; they are serious about mission, strategy, execution, and serving people, but not about their role, image, or themselves.

**6. Develop Mind-Body Awareness:** Most of us are stuck in our heads. We need to pay more attention to our body's messages. Our body reflects everything that's going on in our lives. It is our primary feedback mechanism to reveal the positive or negative impact of our thoughts, emotions, or choices. Start listening to the wisdom of the body. It speaks through energy. *Translation:* Do more of that! It talks through fatigue: *Translation:* Cut down on that and give me more rest! It sends painful messages. *Translation:* I've been warning you gently, but since you ignored me, I will talk a lot louder. Stop doing that! Developing awareness of how the mind affects the body and how the body affects the mind is a crucial skill. Fostering mind-body awareness can be one of our most healing and energizing inside-out competencies.

**7. Manage Stress More Effectively:** Stress is a totally subjective reality. If two people are stressed the same way, one may collapse and the other may thrive on the challenging opportunity. Stress is determined by how we process our world. I recently experienced this first-hand while on a consulting trip in London and Paris. I arrived at the airport late for the flight and got onto the plane as the doors were sealed. To collect myself, I went to the restroom, and since it was occupied, I stood outside, took a deep breath and paused. Suddenly, inside the tiny restroom, I heard a tremendous struggle going on with crashes and pounding noises. My first thought was that someone was having a seizure or heart attack. Just as I was about to get some help, the door flew open. A man, severely physically handicapped with crutches attached to each arm stood before me. Because his legs were paralyzed they swung around following the movement of his contorted upper body. In the midst of his noisy struggle to exit the cramped quarters, he looked at me with a knowing smile and said, "I'm just a butterfly freeing myself from my cocoon!" It was a wonderful moment that I will never forget. If only we all could "process our world" with similar dignity, heart, and resilience.

> *Learn to unclutter your mind. Learn to simplify your work . . . , your work will become more direct and powerful.*
>
> — John Heider

One of my colleagues, Janet Feldman, has developed a "CIA Model" to "process our world" by discerning among three things:

- What Can We *Control*?
- What Can We *Influence*?
- What Must We *Accept*?

Each time you face a stressful situation or event, achieve balance by asking yourself, "What can I *control* in this situation? What can I do to *influence* this situation? What do I have to *accept* here?" Distress is usually the by-product of wasting energy by trying to control things we can only influence or accept, or accepting things we could influence or control. Take action on what you can control or influence and more clearly face what you have to accept.

**8. Nurture Your Close Relationships:** Few things in life can instantaneously balance us as quickly as love. A difficult, stressful day can quickly be put in perspective by the innocence and pure love of a child. Few people could help us to sort out a difficult situation like a supportive spouse or friend. Close relationships can be our anchors in the sea of change. But this "closeness" does not come *from* others to us. It originates as intimacy with ourselves first. We can only give what we have. If our emotional bank account is low, no spending is possible. The key is to develop emotional equity with ourselves first. Then, we will be able to be there for others in their time of need. Likewise, they will be there for us. Sooner or later, we will need to take an "emotional loan" from one of our close relationships to balance our life account.

To help a CEO understand the value of life's most essential relationships, his spouse advised him, "A few years after you leave your job most people will forget you, but your family will always remember you." Chairman and CEO of Novartis, Dr. Daniel Vasella, gave this advice to business school graduates: "Be yourself and don't try to play a role. Tough days never last forever and after follows the good days. Your family and friends will support you in difficult times. Therefore, understand and respect also their needs and strike the right balance for yourself and for them."

**9. Simplify Your Life:** Will Rogers certainly captured how we can complicate our lives unnecessarily when he wrote, "Too many people spend money they haven't earned, to buy things they don't need, to impress the people they don't like." The more we have been living from the outside-in, the more complicated and imbalanced our lives become. The harder we strive to improve *the things* in our lives, the more complex our lives become. As Lily Tomlin has said, "The trouble with the rat race is that even if you win, you're still the rat!"

What are the underlying principles for simplifying life? Sort out *needs vs. wants* and connect with your purpose. Understanding and living our lives consistent with what is really important to us is the process needed to get back to basics. Ask yourself these three crucial questions:

- Is it possible that focusing on satisfying my wants (vs. needs) is complicating my life unnecessarily?
- Is my pursuit of wants taking me away from the life I really hope to live?
- Am I living on-purpose?

If any of the answers is no, don't panic. Feel relieved that you finally see things more clearly, and remind yourself that you don't have to change everything immediately. Take some small steps. Start to rearrange your finances. Make more values-based purchasing decisions. In *The Law of Success*, Paramahansa Yogananda once wrote, "The problem in life is not possessions. The question is, do the possessions support your purpose?" Commit to the process of sorting out your *wants vs. needs*. Begin to simplify your life by making more choices that support the vision of the life you really want to live.

**10. Take Real Vacations:** How often have we gone on a vacation only to return more tired and worn-out than when we left? As fun as it is to expand our boundaries by experiencing new places, does it provide us with the restorative energy we need? Instead of "emptying our bucket," we fill it up with even more stimulation and activity. Why not try a real vacation next time? Why not get some real rest to provide some life perspective? Some of the best examples of real vacations:

- Go to a health spa. Taking a few days for good food, massage, and rest can turn you around. If you can't actually travel to a spa, consider creating your own spa by unplugging the TV, getting more rest, taking a long walk, getting a massage, reading, or journaling your latest aspiration.

- Go on a retreat. Transform your perspective via the gentle, quiet routine of a spiritual or personal retreat. Don't go on a retreat that fills up your day with activities. To advance, you may need to retreat first.

- Go on a vacation by yourself. If your spouse or significant other is secure enough to let you go, it can be a great way to reconnect. There must be a special place you'd love to go.

- Stay at home for a week. Some of my best, most refreshing vacations have been staying at home. If you travel a lot, this can be the most luxurious way to get away.

Try one of these options for your next vacation and recognize the resilience effects over a period of months.

**11. Integrate More Reflection and Introspection into Your Lifestyle:** As leaders, how often do we take time to reflect? In spite of the fact that we are the strategic thinkers behind our organizations, how often do we really step back to re-think ourselves, our lives, and our organizations? On this subject Larry Perlman, former Chairman and CEO of Ceridian, explained, "I would rather have a senior executive go on a weekend of personal reflection than go to another leadership seminar. Leadership is not about learning theory. It's about finding out how you are going to bring yourself into your work and into your life to make a contribution."

If we aspire to do more, then we must be more. Taking time to reflect, taking time to be, is crucial to leaders. It is the still point that everything else revolves around. The more dynamic and effective we want to be in outer life, the more still and composed we need to be within. The more dynamic the system in nature, the more silent the interior. The eye of the hurricane is silent and still—the center of all the energy. The ancient text *The Bhagavad-Gita* captures the essence of resilience: "Established in Being, perform service." This is what real balance and real purpose are all about.

Consider integrating meditation, reflection, prayer, reading, journaling, music, nature, and any other process that brings energy to your dynamic life.

> *What is without periods of rest will not endure.*
> — Ovid

# REFLECTION

## BUILDING ENERGY AND RESILIENCE

Step out of the hurried, hectic pace of life. Let these questions guide you to committing yourself to practices that will enhance your energy and resilience.

1. What can you do to improve the quality of your activity or reduce the quantity to bring more resilience to your lifestyle?

2. What can you do to improve the quality of your rest to revitalize yourself?

3. What habits do you need to replace with more positive behaviors?

4. What are your internal motivators for achieving more resilience?

5. What are your external motivators for achieving more resilience?

6. What is your vision of the more resilient life you want to live?

7. How is your pursuit of wants vs. needs unnecessarily complicating your life and taking you away from your life vision?

8. What is your plan to build more energy?

# LEADERSHIP GROWTH PLAN

## RESILIENCE MASTERY

Take some time now to invest in your energy and resilience. Consider the positive impact the conscious choices you make will have on all aspects of your life. Reflect on "How can I restore and build my energy?" If you want to take it a step further, create another plan for how you will enhance the energy and resilience of your team and organization.

1. Areas for Building Awareness:

   - _____
   - _____
   - _____

2. New Commitments to Make:

   - _____
   - _____
   - _____

3. New Practices to Begin:

   - _____
   - _____
   - _____

4. Potential Obstacles:

   - _____
   - _____
   - _____

5. Timeline and Measures of Success:

   - _____
   - _____
   - _____

# CHAPTER SIX

# BEING MASTERY

## *Leading with Presence*

Being is our essence, the source of our character, the core of who we are. Being supports and drives all our energy, achievement, effectiveness, and contribution. Accessing and expressing Being—our innermost Self—is a key to leading with presence, authenticity, and dynamism. Although this may be unfamiliar territory to many people, we can learn practices for leading from this deepest presence.

## PERSONAL JOURNEY INTO BEING

Exploring Being is an ongoing journey that is particularly helpful to *Leadership from the Inside Out*. Early in my life, I learned to explore Being through meditation. Although meditation is a technique that works for me, it certainly is not the only one. Meditation is only one way. Many other ways are just as effective and easily accessible to us in our everyday lives. We will consider some of these in this chapter, as we have throughout the book. Regardless of the technique or techniques we choose, it's important to understand that these practices are merely bridges to opening ourselves up, "paying attention," as scientist and author Jon Kabat-Zinn would say, and accessing deeper, more silent levels of ourselves.

For several months in 1972, I lived in a small room on the Atlantic coast. At least, that's the superficial description of what I was doing there. What I really was doing was non-doing. I was learning to go into the silence of Being.

Looking back, this was one of the most intense, valuable experiences of my life. Although I didn't comprehend it fully at the time, I was fostering an inner silence that would last a lifetime. I was learning to be present with Self.

Day after day, week after week, month after month, I explored the depths of consciousness. This journey took me so deeply into silence and stillness that after the third week my pulse dropped to 32 beats per minute while my eyes were open! The combination of inner wakefulness and physical rest was transformative. For the first time in my life, I comprehended that life evolves from the inside-out. I was aware of how my fears and anxieties were created

> *Within you there is a stillness and sanctuary to which you can retreat at anytime and be yourself.*
> — The Dhammapada

within. I experienced inner blocks, and I learned to free myself from them to permit energy to flow naturally. I discovered a new type of happiness, one that was unattached to any external event or object. Stress, fatigue, and tension were dissolved by the profound restfulness of going within. It became much clearer to me how life is created within and projected outside.

During this meditation course our group gathered each evening with our teacher, Maharishi Mahesh Yogi. He encouraged us to share our experiences and to ask questions. Spending my days immersed in exploring these inner depths was a rare and wonderful opportunity. Con-

> *Real glory springs from the silent conquest of ourselves.*
> — Joseph Thompson

versing in the evenings with such a wise teacher was pure magic. The sessions were free flowing. We covered everything from the purpose of life, to higher states of consciousness, to the meaning of spirituality. I particularly remember one evening when Maharishi was guiding us through how the inner life supports the outer, and he said, "The son of a millionaire is not born to be poor. Man is born to enjoy. He's born of Bliss, of Consciousness, of Wisdom, of Creativ-

ity. It's a matter of choice whether we shiver in the cold on the verandah or are happy in the warmth of the living room. As long as the outer life is connected with the inner values of Being, then all the avenues of outer life will be rich and glorious." Insight and wisdom like this filled those evenings during which I received more practical and integrative knowledge crucial to success than I learned during my entire academic career.

## GOING TO ANOTHER LEVEL TO RESOLVE LEADERSHIP CHALLENGES

Being present with deeper levels of ourselves to comprehend all sorts of life situations is so natural a process, we may not even be aware of it. Have you ever had the experience of losing your car keys, running frantically around the house, checking over and over all the common places you put them? Exasperated, you give up, sit down, and close your eyes to compose yourself. In this easy, free state of mind, the obscure location of the keys appears. Similarly, have you ever anguished over a very complex problem, and while you're out for a walk in a relaxed state the solution rolls out at your feet?

Recently, I was coaching Laura, a CEO who was exceptionally effective in getting results. The idea of going to a deeper level of life by building more silence into her routine was very foreign. Ask anyone—her professional colleagues, family, and friends—and they would tell you, "Laura is a doer." Convinced that her success was all about her steadfast march toward getting more and more done, she became irritated and dismissive of my suggestion that she incorporate some reflection time, or pauses, into her hectic schedule. She countered, "I don't need to pause more; I need to do more." One day when Laura came in for coaching, she seemed distracted, uncomfortable. When I asked if she had something on her mind, she said, "I don't know what happened today. I was completely stumped after struggling with a chronically tough issue. Instead of going another round, I decided to take a break before coming to see you. I went home and took my dog for a walk through the park. I wasn't thinking about anything. I was just happy to be outside, moving, and breathing the fresh air. Suddenly in a flash, the solution came to me. I was shocked. Where did it come from?"

Like flashes of intuitive insight, awareness of Being, peace, spirit, or whatever we may wish to call it comes to us in a quiet moment. It appears in the silence between our thoughts—the space between the problems and analysis. As we go within, the power of thought is greater. Just as atomic levels are more powerful than molecular levels, our deeper levels of thought have more energy and power. The third law of thermodynamics elucidates this natural flow of energy and power: As activity decreases, order increases. As the mind settles down, it becomes more orderly, more able to comprehend and to handle difficult challenges. As a result, we are able to go beyond the individual issues, combine seemingly unrelated variables, and come up with new solutions or perspectives.

If leadership is the act of going beyond what is, as we have stated earlier in this book, it begins by going beyond what is within ourselves. The inward journey to the center, to the silent experience of Being is "Purpose with a capital *P*." You may be thinking, this is way too esoteric. But, it's not. Far from esoteric, it may be the most practical, grounding force we can have as people and as leaders. David Rock, author of *Quiet Leadership*, and Jeffrey Schwartz, scientist and author of *The Mind and the Brain: Neuroplasticity and the Power of Mental Force*, tell us that meditation and other reflective practices are forms of "regular sustained attention." Scientist Richard Davidson has compared the brains of Tibetan monks, who are veteran meditators, with the brains of first-year college students and found them markedly different. Research done with pilot groups who studied and practiced Mindfulness Meditation for as little as eight weeks showed a significant increase in focusing attention longer and more quickly when distracted as opposed to a control group, who did not receive training. Rock and Schwartz tell us that deeper self-awareness and quieting the mind, especially the amygdala region, which is stimulated by stress,

> *No amount of human having or human doing can make up for a deficit in human being.*
> — John Adams

increases the functioning of the prefrontal cortex, the analytical, processor region of the brain, which neuroscientist and author (with Craig Pearson) of *Upgrading the Executive Brain: Breakthrough Science and Technology of Leadership* Alarik Arenander, Ph.D., calls the "CEO of the brain." This is certainly not a new or exotic idea. Blaise Pascal, the French philosopher and mathematician, wrote, "All men's miseries derive from not being able to sit quietly in a room alone."

Maharishi Mahesh Yogi, the founder of Transcendental Meditation, has said, "The genius of man is hidden in the silence of his awareness, in that settled state of mind, from where every thought emerges. . . . This is not the inert silence of a stone, but a creative silence where all possibilities reside."

Over the years, we have come up with a progressive formula that connects silence to leadership. With no silence, there is no reflection. With no reflection, there is no vision. With no vision, there is no leadership. As counterintuitive as it may seem, silence and reflection are actually performance pathways to more expanded vision and more effective, innovative leadership.

In the book *Presence: An Exploration of Profound Change in People, Organizations and Societies*, Peter Senge, C. Otto Scharmer, Joseph Jaworski, and Betty Sue Flowers—co-authors—consider why it is so difficult for people to effect change. Interviews with over 150 leading scientists, social leaders, and entrepreneurs contributed to the authors' conclusion that we need the ability to view familiar problems from a new perspective in order to better understand how parts and wholes are related. Senge and the others discuss why it is essential to step back to get a much larger perspective of the whole. "When the experience of the past isn't helpful . . . a new kind of learning is needed." They tell us that "presencing is when we retreat and reflect . . . [and thereby] allow inner knowing to emerge." Only after that can we "act swiftly with a natural flow." Cultivating a deeper awareness, an inner knowing through the reflective practices of exploring Being, can support the confidence and fluidity needed to lead beyond the known to the unknown. In *Presence*, Scharmer points to something economist Brian Arthur said in an interview: "Managers think that a fast decision is what counts. If the situation is new, slowing down is necessary. . . . Then act fast and with a natural flow that comes from the inner knowing. You have to slow down long enough to really see what's needed."

David Rock and Jeffrey Schwartz tell us that "moments of insight," what I would call flashes of intuitive insight, need to be fostered in leaders at all levels of an organization. This "new kind of knowing" comes from a deeper awareness and requires non-doing . . . a profound quieting.

## GETTING THINGS DONE BY NON-DOING

The toughest problems we face are rarely solved on their own level. Ken Brousseau and Addy Chulef of Decision Dynamics tell us that "leaders need to understand context, business meaning, complexities, and unkowns, while listening openly, all the while keeping a 'true north' and being able to flex within it." The mind needs to go to a more profound, more comprehensive level. It never ceases to amaze me how much "work" we can get done by "non-work." For most leaders, the most innovative ideas and creative solutions usually arise, not during traditional work hours, but during the quiet, inner moments while swimming, running, walking, gardening, or meditating. The mind is loose, settled, relaxed, and able to comprehend the parts and the whole at the same time. In a *Fortune* commentary on CNNMoney.com dated March 2006, Anne Fisher writes in support of time to reflect: "What scientists have only recently begun to realize is that people may do their best thinking when they are not concentrating on work at all." Fisher cites Dutch psychologists in the journal *Science*, who say, "The unconscious mind is a terrific solver of complex problems when the conscious mind is busy elsewhere or, perhaps better yet, not overtaxed at all." The president of a consumer products firm related to me how his daily swims were "Zen-like experiences where I peacefully sort out very difficult and complex issues. I don't even go to the pool to 'do' anything. It just happens when I get into that calm, yet aware state." In the *Fortune* article just mentioned, Fisher reminds us that Archimedes discovered the principle of displacement while "lolling in his bathtub." As Wolfgang Amadeus Mozart wrote, "When I am, as it were, completely myself, entirely alone, and of good cheer—say traveling in a carriage or walking after a good meal . . . it is on such occasions that ideas flow best and most abundantly."

## THE SEARCH FOR SOMETHING MORE

As leaders, how often do we take the time to relax and to think? Our job is to be above and beyond the daily grind, but often we are immersed in only the doing. Can leaders expect to be ahead of the strategic curve when we rarely get a chance to catch our breath and think in new ways?

> *The soul will bring forth fruit exactly in the measure in which the inner life is developed in it. If there is no inner life, however great may be the zeal, the high intention, the hard work, no fruit will come forth.*
>
> — Charles de Foucald

At one time, I was talking to Paul Walsh, CEO of Diageo, about what he thought leaders in the next millennium would require. He quickly responded, "More time to reflect and to think provocatively about current and future dynamics." Another CEO put it this way: "As leaders, our real challenge is to carve out more time to think and more time to be. When we do it, we're more refreshed and more creative. Unfortunately, we get caught up in achieving and sometimes forget where our energy and creativity come from." Leaders are constantly searching for something more. We want more achievement, more happiness, more fulfillment. It is a natural tendency. The crucial thing, however, is how we satisfy this inherent desire for more. Do we attempt to "fill ourselves up" from the outside-in? Or, are we able to give ourselves something really satisfying from the inside-out?

> *I think what we're seeking is an experience of being alive, so that our life experiences on the purely physical plane will have resonances within our innermost Being and reality, so that we actually feel the rapture of being alive.*
>
> — Joseph Campbell

Mastery of Being is that "something more" we can "give" ourselves in a self-sufficient way. It is about learning to transform our state of awareness to greater strength and satisfaction by ourselves. No outside intervention or stimulation is required. We can do it all *by ourselves* with no harmful side effects. Imagine having the power to transform yourself physically and emotionally when you are feeling tired and stressed. That's the power of Being. Imagine problems turning to opportunities, irritation to compassion, and alienation to connection. So, why don't we connect more with this state of Being?

## DON'T PLACE "DESCARTES" BEFORE "THE SOURCE"

Our fast-moving, never-catch-your-breath, externally focused culture is designed "perfectly" to avoid genuine contact with the deeper levels of ourselves. The background and foreground "noise" of our lives is so dominant, we rarely get a chance to connect with any silence within us. In fact, we have become so stimulation-oriented that even our "fun" and "happiness" have become associated with ever-increasing high doses of artificial distraction. Most people go on vacations and have so much *fun* that they return exhausted! Others strap large rubber bands to themselves and then jump off bridges to experience "the thrill of living"! Although fun, work, achievement, play, and exhilaration are all important parts of a fulfilling life, too often these experiences are an addictive search for the next stimulating experience to fill the void inside. We become "junkies" to external stimulation, always seeking our next "fix" to make us feel good. The proliferation and easy access to increasingly tiny, wireless electronic devices designed to save us time and to entertain us contribute to lives in which we are connected to everything else but ourselves. This type of "I'm stimulated, therefore I am" mentality often lacks the true joy of living. We have become a world of *human doers* having lost connection to our heritage as *human beings*.

Leaders probably would agree with Descartes: "I think, therefore I am." But Being Mastery has a different view: "I am, therefore I think." To be alive, to be effective, to be fulfilled, first requires a state of Being. Therefore, Mastery of Being does not place "Descartes" before the "Source."

Thinking is the effect; Being is the cause. Being is consciousness in its pure form, the source of thought. It is not a thought; it is the source of thought. It is not an experience; it is experience itself. In *No Man Is an Island*, Thomas Merton wrote:

> We are warmed by fire, not by the smoke of the fire. We are carried over the sea by ship, not by the wake of a ship. So too, what we are is sought in the depths of our own Being, not in our outward reflection of our own acts. We must find our real selves not in the froth stirred up by the impact of our Being upon the beings or things around us, but in our own Being which is the principle of all our acts.

> I do not need to see myself, I merely need to be myself. I must think and act like a living Being, but I must not plunge my whole self into what I think and do.

People who project themselves entirely into activity, and seek themselves entirely outside themselves, are like madmen who sleep on the sidewalk in front of their houses instead of living inside where it is quiet and warm.

## TECHNIQUES TO UNFOLD BEING

To understand the practical relationship of Being in our lives, we need to look at our everyday experience. Most of us would agree that successful action is based on effective thinking. If our thoughts are clear and focused, then our actions will be precise and effective. But on the days we do not feel well, our thoughts are less effective and our actions less successful. So feeling is more fundamental than thinking; feeling gives rise to thinking, which gives rise to action. Feeling, thinking, and action all have one thing in common—they are always changing. Sometimes we feel great, think clearly, and act effectively. Other times, we do not. But feeling, thinking, and action all have one non-changing "thing" in common—Being. To feel, to think, to act, we first must Be. The pure state of Being underlies all areas of life. The more we awaken our true nature—Being—the more effective our feeling, thinking, and action. It is the foundation, the platform for a more masterful life.

> *Compared to what we ought to be, we are half awake.*
> —William James

Another practical way to understand the value of Being is in terms of the different states of consciousness. Typically we experience three states of consciousness: waking, dreaming, and deep sleep. Each state of consciousness has a unique state of measurable physiological functioning. The same goes for dreaming and deep sleep. Being is a distinctly different state of consciousness—a fourth major state. It's a state of restful alertness where the mind is fully awake in its own nature and the body is deeply rested, even more profoundly than during deep sleep. As we stretch the mind and body to experience broader ranges of their potentialities, we eventually acquire the natural experience of Being or Pure Consciousness permeating the other three states of consciousness. As a result, we truly begin to live life from the inside-out. Every experience we have is in the context of our awakened inner nature.

So how does one experience Being? There are as many paths to experience Being as there are people. Some experience it through meditation, some through prayer, others through nature, and for others it comes naturally. Franz Kafka wrote:

> You need not do anything; you need not leave your room. Remain sitting at your
> table and listen. You don't even need to wait; just become still, quiet, and solitary,
> and the world will freely offer itself to you to be unmasked. It has no choice; it will
> roll in ecstasy at your feet.

Abraham Maslow, in *Toward a Psychology of Being*, found that self-actualized people had a high frequency of such "peak experiences." These experiences were described as moments of great awe, pure positive happiness, when all doubts, all fears, all inhibitions, all weaknesses, were left behind. They felt one with the world, pleased with it, really belonging to it, instead of being outside looking in—they had the feeling that they had really seen the truth, the essence of things. Maslow identified 14 recurring themes or "values of Being" experienced by self-actualized people:

- Wholeness
- Perfection
- Completion
- Justice
- Aliveness
- Richness
- Simplicity

- Beauty
- Goodness
- Uniqueness
- Effortlessness
- Playfulness
- Truth
- Self-Sufficiency

Unless these values are an everyday experience for us, we will need some assistance in gaining insights into Being. Although there are many other techniques, one of the best ways I have found is through meditation. Since meditation simply means "to think," or as Jon Kabat-Zinn says, to "pay attention," all of us meditate. To arrive at a pure state of Being, we want to learn how to go beyond our thoughts—to transcend meditation. Meditation is a technique for helping us arrive at this state naturally.

I've practiced many forms of meditation over the years. My personal preference is the Transcendental Meditation (TM) program. It's *not* the only way to meditate, just one way that has worked well for me and many others. I was attracted to it because it was easy to learn and didn't require any belief or behavior changes. I also liked the fact that it was one of the most thoroughly researched human development programs, with more than 600 research studies documenting its benefits to mind, body, and behavior. Among those studies is research to support reduction in cortisol (a stress hormone), muscle tension, high blood pressure, serum cholesterol, hypertension, and anxiety. Studies show that for people who practice Transcendental Meditation, "Hospitalization is 87 percent lower for heart disease . . . and meditators over 40 years old have approximately 70 percent fewer medical problems than others in their age group."

Another form, Mindfulness Meditation, and a program called *Mindfulness-Based Stress Reduction (MBSR)*, developed by Jon Kabat-Zinn, are gaining widespread acceptance and are being taught in a range of settings all over the world. Ten to 15 years ago this was almost unheard of. The *MBSR* program blends meditation and other techniques with daily practices for living mindfully, in the present moment. Abundant research and experience with *MBSR* indicates reduced stress and relief from chronic pain and depression, as well as a beneficial influence on the immune system. Paul Erdahl, Vice President of Executive and Leadership Development at Medtronic, Inc., said that Bill George, former CEO, created a culture at Medtronic in which meditation was comfortable and encouraged. He also said that although their leadership development programs do not include meditation practice, they do include many tools and opportunities for reflection. *Introduction to Mindfulness Meditation* is offered to employees through the Work-Life Employee Assistance Program (EAP) at Medtronic. Steve Clark, an EAP psychologist, says employees on all levels take the course, and many participants repeat. The most common feedback is that they feel "more focused." According to David Rock and Jeffrey Schwartz, "Meditation helps the brain overcome the urge to automatically respond to external events," a skill that is vitally important to leaders at all levels given the barrage of distractions in daily life.

The practical value of meditation can best be understood in terms of its profound rest. Every night when we sleep, we leave the field of activity, close our eyes, and "transcend" our daytime activity. This settling down of mental and physical activity results in rest and stress relief, which prepares us for dynamic action the next day. Profound meditation is similar with one major difference: We maintain our awareness as we experience inordinately deep rest. We experience a state of restful alertness where the mind is alert but settled, and the body is deeply rested, even more completely rested than during sleep. When we open our eyes, we feel revitalized, think more clearly, and act more effectively. When we learn to settle into our Being, we naturally become more and more ourselves. It is much like the experience of taking a refreshing bath. If the bath is truly refreshing, you are refreshed. You don't have to convince yourself you are refreshed; you do not have to create a mood of being refreshed. You don't have to believe you are refreshed. *You are refreshed.* This is not the power of positive thinking. It is the power of Positive Being. As William Penn wrote, "True Silence is the rest of the mind; it is to the spirit what sleep is to the body, nourishment and refreshment."

# REFLECTION

## EXPLORING THE LEADER WITHIN

Take a little break now to explore the leader within. The following reflection is not related to doing Transcendental Meditation or applying any other formal meditation technique. It is just meant to be a small taste—an *hors d'oeuvres* of going within. If you want the full meal, you may want to consider personal meditation instruction.

Find a quiet place and sit comfortably. Close your eyes. Stretch your body so it loosens and relaxes. Let your awareness follow the flow of your breathing, in and out. When your mind wanders, gently come back to your breathing. Observe your awareness settling down. Let your thoughts, sensations, anxieties, and worries appear as if on a large screen. Let your thoughts come and go. Just return to your breathing. If your awareness of the breathing starts to fade, just let your awareness fade. No need to force anything. No need to resist anything. No need to do anything. Just be aware of the entire process in a non-judging manner. If the "bottom drops out" and you find yourself thinking again, you may have just transcended into Being. Just return your awareness gently to your breathing. After 15–20 minutes, lie down for five minutes and then slowly get up. Notice how this calm, centered, refreshed state of awareness could be brought forth into your leadership . . . and life.

## CONNECTING WITH OUR INNER SELF

Several years ago, I gave a lecture entitled "Meditation and the Dynamic Life" at a university. This well-attended event attempted to present new paradigms about meditation as preparation for an effective life vs. a retreat from life. The audience had so many misconceptions about meditation requiring concentration or contemplation or withdrawal from the world that the lecture went longer than expected. Since I had to speak at another event that evening and I had a long distance to travel, I cut short some of the questions, packed my car, and began my drive. Before too long, it occurred to me that if I wanted to be "at my best" for this next lecture, I needed to refresh myself. So, I pulled the car over near a dense woods. I left the car, found a soft, mossy spot, and I meditated. As my mind and body repeatedly dove into and out of deep restfulness, my freshness, clarity, and vitality returned.

> *There is one means of procuring solitude which to me, and I apprehend all men, is effectual, and that is to go to a window and look at the stars. If they do not startle you and call you off from vulgar matters, I know not what will.*
>
> — Ralph Waldo Emerson

As I was about to open my eyes and return to the car, I heard footsteps. Cracking my eyes open, I saw a large buck three to four feet away stomping his hoof and waving his head back and forth. While I was enjoying his display, a second, third, and fourth deer joined us. Before returning to the car, I enjoyed 10 to 15 minutes of observing these magnificent forest creatures, who didn't seem the least uncomfortable in my presence. Refreshed and renewed through my meditation, I continued my drive and arrived at my next presentation feeling revitalized. That is why connection with Being is a wonderful preparation for action. It is also a great preparation for seeing life with new eyes. As Marcel Proust wrote, "The real voyage of discovery consists not in seeing new landscapes, but in having new eyes."

Although meditation is a great way to connect with our inner potentiality, it is not the only way. Meditation is a technique to bring our mind from the surface of life to the depths of Being. What are some other techniques? Since we're talking about a level of life that is at the basis of all our experiences, we have the potential to locate that level in any experience. So, what are the best ways to do this? I am sure you have your own paths to Being, but here are a few that work well for many:

- *Reverence for Nature*
  Most of us at some time in our lives have become overwhelmed by the immensity and grandeur of nature. When we stare into the heavens on a star-filled night, gaze over

the Grand Canyon, snorkel through tropical waters, or walk along a creek in our neighborhood, we experience a *moment of awe* beyond our intellectual comprehension. David Whyte, the poet and motivational speaker, suggests that "what we find in nature is the intuitive knowledge that it might be possible to rest into ourselves, to be still." That moment of deep, silent, unbounded appreciation beyond and between our thoughts is the experience of inner Being. Spend time in nature and enjoy the technique of profound appreciation and wonder to stretch or extend your boundaries.

- *Music*
  Music, because it moves us directly and deeply, is probably the most powerful art form. It can open the gateway to one's soul directly with its organized vibrations. The vibrations that move each of us are different. Handel's *Water Music* or Gregorian chants "take me away." Find the music that soothes and relaxes you the most. (I also like the Rolling Stones, but I only listen to them when I want to *express energy* rather than connect with it.) Go deeply into soothing music—it can be a wonderful way to explore your Being. T. S. Eliot wrote, "Music heard so deeply that it is not heard at all. But you are the music while the music lasts."

- *Present-Moment Awareness*
  Rarely comprehending the present moment fully, we often live our lives in the past or the future. Being is infinity contained in the eternally present moment. Thinking about Being in the present is not Being in the present—it is *thinking about* Being in the present. It is not something we can make a mood about. It is only something we can become aware of. When you're late for an appointment, caught in rush-hour traffic, or missing a deadline, catch your stressed state of mind and tune into the present. You will refresh yourself, save wasted energy, and be more effective.

  When you become aware of the silent witness behind all your dynamic activity, Being is present. Gay Hendricks and Kate Ludeman write in *The Corporate Mystic*, "Corporate Mystics put a great deal of attention on learning to be in the present moment because they have found that this is the only place from which time can be expanded. If you are in the present—not caught up in regret about the past or anxiety about the future—time essentially becomes malleable." If we are always effective in the present moment, can effectiveness and fulfillment escape us?

- *Children at Play*

  How deep is the meditation of a child at play? It is pure Being in action. The joy, energy, focus, spontaneity, and vibrancy of children can teach all of us the way to our goal. As John Steinbeck wrote, "Genius is a child chasing a butterfly up a mountain."

- *Love*

  Love is the transcendental glue of the universe. Love unifies and connects everything. It is the vibration of Being in our lives. At the moment of pure love and appreciation, we transcend our limitations and connect with all there is. Love is the road to Being and the road from Being to the world.

- *Traumatic Events*

  As difficult as dramatic changes in our lives are, the trauma of these events can shake us up so much that we cope by letting go of everything that seemed so important. In doing so, we can connect with something deeper within ourselves. Consider being more open to the vulnerability of unexpected changes as a pathway to inner Self.

> *There is no need to go to India to find peace. You will find that deep place of silence right in your room, your garden or even your bathtub.*
>
> — Elizabeth Kübler-Ross

- *Inspirational Reading*

  Reading the accounts of people on their journey to realization can be a helpful aid to us on our path. Even though we're reading about other people's experiences, the insights can be helpful and motivational as we progress. Sometimes they provide clarity and validation. Other times, we learn about an area of personal development we need to explore. Once in a while, we become inspired and awaken our essence.

## BEING AND EXECUTIVE PRESENCE

Many of the executives I have coached over the years have what could be called *unconscious competence* when it comes to the presence of Being. It's unconscious because they aren't aware of it. When I inquire into their experiences of inner silence supporting their effectiveness, they often give me a puzzled look. They may even become very uncomfortable and label such pursuits as "too esoteric or impractical." In spite of this lack of awareness, effective people often have a degree of competence in this area. They have what people call "executive

> *There are only two ways to live your life . . . As though nothing is a miracle . . . or as though everything is a miracle.*
>
> — Albert Einstein

presence"—a solid, confident, calm demeanor not easily shaken by external circumstances. Even though they may be experiencing some of the benefits of Being, they haven't made the connection consciously. Even though they are not fully aware of it, it is their Being—their inner presence—that fosters confidence in others to follow them.

Helping effective people to move from unconscious competence to conscious competence when it comes to Being Mastery is crucial. It is one of the most practical ways to impact effectiveness and fulfillment simultaneously. Devoid of conscious competence, our connection to the benefits of Being is haphazard and sporadic. As a result, we are likely to remain at our current level of realization and thereby limit our external performance. It's much like a naturally talented athlete who needs to become more conscious of his talents and entire life situation to move to the next level. Pausing for Being allows us to play at a new level—the player, the game, and the process of playing are all enhanced permanently. Jim Secord, former CEO of Lakewood Publications and Publisher of *Training* magazine, sees the practical benefits of grounding himself in these principles. Reflecting on the most challenging times in his career, he said, "Had I been unable to ground myself in spiritual principles and practices during the tough times, I wouldn't have been able to rise up to the challenges of leadership."

## LEADERSHIP BENEFITS OF BEING

Being is the soul of leadership; it is spirit expressing itself through the leader. If you have had the good fortune to be in the presence of leaders such as Nelson Mandela, Jimmy Carter, Maya Angelou, or the Dalai Lama, you probably have walked away moved by their sense of peacefulness and joy. The transcendental quality of their silence makes everything they say resound more deeply and clearly in our hearts. This palpable sense of tranquility that is untouched even by very stressful or life-threatening circumstances is the essence of effective leadership.

One of the Dalai Lama's monks, who had been imprisoned and tortured for years by the Chinese after their takeover of Tibet, was interviewed during a visit to Minneapolis. The reporter asked the calm, peaceful monk what he had feared most during his years of abuse. He responded honestly and humbly. "I was most afraid that I would lose my compassion for the Chinese." It was a stunning moment, rich with heart, spirit, and learning for everyone present; this is Being in action.

Individuals who have taken the journey to this level of personhood are not only leaders of people and causes, but leaders of life. They are the ones committed to leading our world to

*Sometimes I sits and thinks,*
*and sometimes I just sits.*
— Satchel Paige

a more enriching future, and they are the ones who, by virtue of who they are, can truly honor that commitment. Attaining this level of development, however, need not be the exclusive domain of a few. It is waiting for all of us; it is at the core of who we are.

As leaders, what are some of the practical benefits of bringing the awareness of Being to our conscious, everyday experience?

- Our inner calm attracts others to us. People are more comfortable with our increasingly peaceful yet dynamic presence. People tend to seek out our thoughtful advice and counsel.
- We are better equipped to deal with rapid change around us because we are more calm and centered within.
- Our drive for external success is enhanced by our awareness of deeper, more fundamental values. As a result, our external success has more meaning, context, and depth.
- We can solve tough, challenging problems more easily. Our minds can get above, below, and around seemingly difficult situations.
- The profound rest of Being gives us the ability to refresh ourselves and allows us to achieve more with less effort.
- More life balance is achieved because we have the energy and calmness to cope dynamically with life challenges. People sense our balance and trust our thoughtful, calm demeanor.
- We have the distinct sense that we are growing to become more uniquely and authentically ourselves. Qualities of character flow through us more often and more naturally.

If we want to do more, we first need to be more. As Emerson wrote, "We but half express ourselves, and are ashamed of that divine which each of us represents." Take more time to reflect and to be. Since leaders lead by virtue of who they are, commit to expanding the depth of your character to its most essential level—Being.

# FOUR POINTS OF AWARENESS FOR LEADING WITH PRESENCE

Keep the following points in mind as you begin to master leading with presence:

*1. Take Your Own Journey into Being:* Find your own path to unfold Being. It's your road, and only you can travel it. Only you can judge what "vehicles" will help you on your journey. Consider meditation, prayer, reflection, music, nature, and any other "techniques" that seem to resonate with you. Start walking, and the journey is half over.

*2. Resolve Life Challenges by Going to a Deeper Level:* Problems are rarely solved on their own level. Learn to go to a deeper level to view things in a more comprehensive way. As your mind learns to settle down yet remain alert, the ability to sort through and to organize your life will be amazing. Understand the power of non-doing—those uniquely open, relaxed moments when the complex becomes simple, and the unsolvable is solved.

*3. Consider Learning to Meditate:* At least consider the possibility of learning to meditate properly. It may be the best investment in your development you ever make. If you have a particularly strong resistance to spending time with yourself in reflection or meditation, then the need to do so is probably great. Allow the resistance to be there, but still spend the time to do it. As you experience the benefits, the resistance will subside.

*4. Integrate Some Reflection into Your Life:* Getting on the path to Being involves committing to a lifestyle that values more solitude, reflection, and meditation. Take some "Being Breaks" by investing some time getting reacquainted with yourself. Enjoy the solitude. Go on some walks. Sort out your priorities. Experience the silence. Reducing the "noise" of normal living and spending time in nature can help you to reconnect. Try not to fill up all your time with endless distractions. Don't just do something—sit there! Enjoy the moonlight on the water, the cry of the loon, the scent of pine in the cool air, the crash of the waves. It will settle you down and bring you closer to yourself. But keep in mind this is not an end in itself. It is preparation for a more dynamic, masterful life. It is not an escape, but rather a discovery—a process of finding and connecting with the essence of life.

# LEADERSHIP GROWTH PLAN
## BEING MASTERY

Reflect on the learnings that have surfaced as you read this chapter. Consider some new areas of Awareness, Commitment, and Practice, as well as potential obstacles, resources, and signs or measures of success. Reflect on the question, "How can I bring more peaceful presence into my leadership and my life?"

1. Areas for Building Awareness:

   * _____
   * _____
   * _____

2. New Commitments to Make:

   * _____
   * _____
   * _____

3. New Practices to Begin:

   * _____
   * _____
   * _____

4. Potential Obstacles:

   * _____
   * _____
   * _____

5. Timeline and Measures of Success:

   * _____
   * _____
   * _____

# CHAPTER SEVEN

# ACTION MASTERY

*Leading through Coaching*

*Leadership from the Inside Out* is the ongoing development journey to discover and apply the talents and values that fuel purpose in order to drive a positive impact on the world around us. By incorporating the principles of each mastery area into our lives, we deepen our authenticity, heighten our influence, and increase the value we create. We forge a formidable, yet agile platform from which to learn and to lead. Action Mastery is a continuous process, through coaching ourselves and others, to pull together our potentialities in order to *go beyond what is* . . . inside and out. Paul Reilly, Chairman of Korn/Ferry International, heightens the compelling need to take action to coach and develop key leaders: "In five years, 50 percent of all C-Level executives will retire. Therefore, the need has never been more urgent to cultivate key talent, to make coaching a part of each leader's development plan, and to recognize leadership potential at every level of organizations." As a result, Action Mastery gives us the focused inner and outer plan to serve our constituencies.

As I consider the power of coaching and how much untapped potential we all have, I'm reminded of an experience I had several years ago on Lake Superior. (I know you're thinking, "Can't that guy just stay off that darned lake!") Denise, my former spouse of 20 years and fortunately still my great friend, accompanied me on this trip to the north shore. We were staying in a small, rustic cabin on a cliff overlooking the lake, and we were hoping for waters calm enough to explore the caves and hidden beaches accessible only by water. For three days, we were disappointed; the water was too rough to venture out. On the fourth day, the lake was totally calm—not a ripple to be seen.

Excited, we packed up our gear and headed out onto the placid, smooth lake. We were thrilled to be gliding atop the water on such a perfect day. Our canoeing was effortless and smooth. Peering over the sides of our craft into the chilly depths, we viewed the beautiful yet ominous world that stirred both our curiosity and vulnerability. Seeing the gigantic slabs of rock and boulders polished smooth over thousands of years gave us a fresh, yet eerie perspective. Denise fantasized about draining the lake and exploring the mountains and valleys below. Our first real clearing from the cliffs and rocks came about five miles down the lake

> *We delude ourselves into thinking that it is safer to stay in the zone of the predictable. This, however, can be a bad bargain, especially if we want to go all the way to full success in life. . . . The moment we choose to stay in the predictable zone is the moment we sign our death warrant as a creative individual.*
>
> — Gay Hendricks and
> Kate Ludeman

at a beautiful old lodge. Stopping in the clearing for a leisurely rest, we lay back in the canoe and caught some sunshine for 10 or 15 minutes.

Suddenly a cold wind, not a cool breeze, jolted us from our reverie. I perked up and noticed the flag at the lodge standing straight out—a warning signal. We jumped up, grabbed our paddles, and decided to head back. The lake gradually mustered energy. At first, we joked back and forth about the waves and how fun it was. About a mile and a half out, the jokes were over. We were caught in the wild surges of Superior. Because the waves were breaking so high, the most dangerous areas were closest to the rocky cliffs of the shoreline. We had no choice; we had to keep going out farther into the lake for safety. The swells were so high that Denise's head dropped beneath the top of them. As we descended over the waves, the canoe landed with a loud slap. Realizing we were in a life-or-death situation, we encouraged each other, sometimes in not-so-calm voices, and affirmed our resolve to get through this arduous challenge. While coping with the formidable waves, I lost my life preserver, which hooked itself under our canoe. It not only slowed us down, but if we capsized . . . you get the picture. We just kept going. We got our second winds, third winds, fourth winds. After a while we were definitely in a "zone"—a calm, focused place amidst the raging waters. In fact, we got so absorbed that after four hours of paddling, we actually passed our cabin. Overcome with joy and relief, we glided into our little cove—our haven—and collapsed on the rocks like two exhausted sea lions after a big night of fishing.

> *I know of no more encouraging fact than the unquestionable ability of man to elevate his life by conscious endeavor.*
>
> — Mother Teresa

That evening, as we reflected on the wild day, we were astounded at the levels of inner strength and potentiality we called up. We passed our limits many times. We transcended them so completely that we went to a place of effortlessness, totally unexpected by either of us. How much farther could we have gone? I don't know. All I know is that we went way beyond what we thought was possible.

What is our potentiality for achievement from the inside-out? Does life really have infinite possibilities as the great sages and thinkers have said throughout history? Is our world really a field of all possibilities, teaming with life, energy, and seemingly endless options? Or does our life have a more limited horizon of success and possibility?

Researchers in the neurophysiology of the brain are beginning to give us some profound insights into our real potentiality. Using conservative estimates, researchers have projected that there are 100 trillion neuron junctions in the human brain. That means that our possible mental states are more than the total number of atoms in the universe. Think about that . . . our brain potentially can find more possibilities than there are atoms in the universe. Is it possible for us to comprehend infinity? Maybe. Is our field of possibilities vastly larger than we think? Definitely.

For years, scientists believed the brain's structure was hardwired and couldn't be changed. An abundance of research in the last 10 to 15 years has shown that our brains are much more flexible than previously thought. Scientists in biomedicine, neurology, and psychology are studying the implications of the brain's "plasticity." Sharon Begley, science columnist for *Newsweek,* reports research that has determined that through a process called neurogenesis, we can grow new neurons, we can change our brain cells, and we can change traits of our brain. In her book *Train Your Mind, Change Your Brain*, Begley writes, "The question of whether the brain can change, and whether the mind has the power to change it, is emerging as one of the most compelling of our time." Scientists Richard Davidson, Fred Gage, Helen Neville, Michael Meaney, Daniel Goleman, Jeffrey Schwartz, Jon Kabat-Zinn, and many others in a variety of scientific disciplines are collaborating with each other and the Dalai Lama, who has been encouraging the study of the brains of Tibetan monks to learn more about how meditation, as a form of mental training, does train our minds and change our brains. Begley tells us:

> Davidson's research supports an idea that Buddhist meditation adepts have long maintained: that the mental training that lies at the core of meditative practice can alter the brain and thus the mind in an enduring way—strengthening connection from the thoughtful prefrontal lobes to the fear- and anxiety-generating amygdala, shifting activity in the prefrontal cortex from the discontented right side to the eudaemonic left side. Connection among neurons can be physically modified through mental training just as biceps can be modified by physical training.

> *Awareness without commitment and practice is leadership in adolescence.*
> — Renée Garpestad

The implications of this knowledge for leadership development, Learning Agility, growth, and coaching on all levels are profound. Few would question the far reaches of our potentiality. The real question is, "How well are we using this potential?" Are we playing the concerto of life with one finger? William James wrote, "Most people live, whether physically, intellectually, or morally, in a very restricted circle of their potential being. They make use of a very small portion of their possible consciousness, and of their soul's resources in general, much like a man who, out of his whole bodily organism should opt into a habit of using and moving only his little finger."

*Leadership from the Inside Out* is about playing the song of our life with depth, passion, and world-class skill. How can we ensure that we don't have only an occasional beautiful concert but, instead, gradually become the harmonious melody itself?

## MERGING THREE INTERRELATED ACTION MASTERY STEPS

Coaching ourselves and others is the key to taking action in leadership and catalyzing our fullest potential. All traditions throughout the ages have had exceptional coaches—advisors, sages, elders, wisdom-keepers, teachers, mentors, shamans, gurus, masters—to help people look at their lives and behaviors from new, deeper vantage points. These coaches helped their "coachees"—seekers, disciples, students, apprentices—to see the world with fresh eyes, to know that it is possible to move beyond or transcend what they thought was possible, and to glimpse their fullest potential. This has always been the beginning of the transformational journey for authentic leadership in life.

The best way to take action for ourselves is through coaching. For self-coaching or coaching others to have a lasting, transformative impact, three interrelated pathways need to merge: *Awareness, Commitment,* and *Practice.* If all three are present and operating, breakthroughs will occur and growth will be sustained. If any one of the three is absent, the results will dissipate over time. You may learn the best techniques and disciplines to practice, but if you lack commitment, you won't continue your efforts. Similarly, all the enthusiasm and commitment in the world won't get you far if you don't adhere to a workable action plan. And without awareness of your strengths and weaknesses, how will you know what to commit to or what you need to do?

Not long ago, two executives were referred to us for leadership coaching. They both had about the same level of compensation, and they both had about 20 years of uninterrupted success with *Fortune 500* companies. They both excelled on the job. They both also needed to work on their leadership and interpersonal effectiveness if they wanted to continue to advance in their organizations. Each approached his development in dramatically different ways. One person was open to learning and willing to commit to the growth process from the inside-out. The other person felt that he already "had it all figured out."

At the start of coaching, they both exhibited reasonable willingness. After a few days, one executive lost enthusiasm, as he got closer to some real feedback on his style and personality. He began to regard the process as "lots of work" and would say, "I'm not sure how relevant it is." He began to miss some appointments. As he pulled back, he began to speculate if the program was "worth it." He became increasingly skilled at fulfilling his prophecy and at rationalizing his lack of benefit.

The other person stayed with the program. He threw himself into every coaching session. He indulged himself in the self-exploration. He listened to the feedback and looked for ways to understand and to apply the information to his career, team, and life. He explored deeply his core meaning and purpose. He projected a new vision for a more authentic life and for more authentic leadership, one that was congruent with his real values. He began to read and reflect more. He shared his insights with others. He began to open up with people at work. He began to admit his strengths and weaknesses to others. He began to ask for their help and to value their contributions. He stayed the course. He became a very effective, empowering, agile leader. He was courageous. When the waves became wild and challenging during his own sea change, he paddled harder and stayed focused. He never lost sight of his purpose; he believed he could and would go beyond his limits. He got onto the path of "leadership from the inside-out." Within a year, he was promoted to president of the corporation.

The other person? He was outplaced six months later. He continued the same rigid pattern of not taking responsibility and projecting his limitations externally. He probably still blames his former company for his misfortunes.

Now let's apply the three interrelated steps to Action Mastery—Building Awareness, Building Commitment, and Building Practice to coaching yourself.

## ACTION MASTERY STEP ONE: BUILDING AWARENESS

Since you've taken the journey this far, I'll risk making the assumption that you've built at least some degree of additional self-awareness from your reading and reflection. Maybe you've even experienced some big ones, ones that made you stop and think, nod your head, and wonder what impact they've had. Awareness is the first step on the path of coaching.

> *Leadership is the art of accomplishing more than the science of management says is possible.*
> — Colin Powell

Building Awareness is the process of bringing new information into our field of view. It may include keeping our attention on a newly clarified talent we have brought into focus. Or it may involve the more painful process of acknowledging that a behavior is unintentionally self-defeating or affecting others in a life-damaging way. Awareness encompasses the *inner discipline* of looking within ourselves to shed light on our strengths and our growth challenges, and the *outer discipline* of observing ourselves through our own eyes and the eyes of others, as we engage in making an important behavioral shift.

Consider creating an inventory. In creating your inventory, incorporate any feedback you can think of, including a 360° assessment at work or comments made by people over the years about your strengths, talents, developmental needs, personality, and values. This feedback may have come from colleagues, bosses, people who work for you, friends, or loved ones. It is important not just to try to figure this out yourself but to listen closely to what others say. As we have seen, self-awareness can be enhanced from inside or outside. Typically, there is what is known as a "perception gap" between how we see ourselves and how others see us. Our intention here is to face the truth, to get a clear and complete picture. According to Malcolm Gladwell in *Blink*, if you really want to know how you are presenting yourself to others, ask them to tell you and take an honest look at how you are behaving. This is not just a good psychological exercise; it is crucial for leadership and for peak performance. In his groundbreaking book *Working with Emotional Intelligence*, Daniel Goleman writes, "People who are self aware are also better performers. Presumably their self awareness helps them in a process of continuous improvement. . . . Knowing their strengths and weaknesses and approaching their work accordingly, was a competence found in virtually every star performer in a study of several hundred professionals at companies including AT&T and 3M."

Building Awareness requires the willingness to hold a mirror up and take an honest look. This is an act requiring courage. To see, to acknowledge, and to embrace both the positive and negative aspects of who we are demands ongoing bravery. But it is well worth the effort. As the French writer Anaïs Nin said, "Life shrinks or expands in proportion to one's courage." As leaders, our impact shrinks or expands in direct relationship to how well we courageously look at our whole selves—light and shadow. *Building Awareness is the path of courage.*

# REFLECTION

## BUILDING AWARENESS

Take some time to reflect on the awareness you've experienced while reading the previous chapters. Review each mastery area. What were the key learnings in each one? Which awareness theme was the most significant?

If you want to take further action, make an inventory of your strengths and weaknesses as a leader in your team, organization, and family. Look back on your life, and do your best to capture and to include in your inventory your finest achievements as well as your less than stellar moments. Note the activities and aspects of life where you excel, where things go easily for you and flow effortlessly toward success and fulfillment, as well as difficult situations in personal relationships and at work, where you struggle and bump into recurring problems, where you just can't seem to achieve the desired goal. These all shed light on who you are, what your capabilities are, and where you may be in need of some work.

## ACTION MASTERY STEP TWO: BUILDING COMMITMENT

Awareness opens the doorway to higher levels of performance. However, awareness by itself is not enough. To move toward enduring leadership effectiveness requires motivation born of emotional commitment. Building Commitment begins with comprehending the consequences of our actions. However, it is not enough only to understand *intellectually*

*Nothing in the world can take the place of persistence. Talent will not; nothing is more common than unsuccessful men with talent. Genius will not; unrewarded genius is almost a proverb. Education will not; the world is full of educated derelicts. Persistence and determination alone are omnipotent.*

— Calvin Coolidge

that if we continue on the same course, we're going to fall short of our goals, hurt ourselves or others. We have to *feel* it. When we have a deep emotional connection to the impact of a behavior, our life can change permanently. This is why trauma can be such a great change-producing teacher. Noel Tichy and Warren Bennis put it this way: "Courageous leaders often get their courage from their fear about what will happen if they don't step up and boldly step out." I have seen executives repeatedly ignore their fitness and self-care needs until they were in a hospital bed fighting for their lives. Once we clearly perceive and emotionally experience both the upside and downside consequences of a behavior, meaningful commitment to transformation—"boldly stepping out"—can begin.

It is important to recognize the consequences of any life-damaging behaviors we may have, but it is equally valuable to understand the life-enriching benefits of doing something more, less, or differently. Motivation happens when we emotionally experience the compelling, positive reasons to do something, as well as the painful reasons to avoid the downside consequence. Both must be apparent to foster the creative tension necessary to sustain our motivation. What will we gain? What could we lose? Reflecting at the decisive intersection of these opposing consequences gets us to take action.

# REFLECTION

## BUILDING COMMITMENT

If you would like to begin strengthening your commitment muscle, try this exercise. Start by deciding what commitments you are willing to make around the greatest awareness you've had since reading this book, the one you identified in the Building Awareness exercise.

Ready to go to another level? Identify several things you would like to do more, less, or differently in order to improve your life and leadership effectiveness. Make a list of the most important items, and from this list, pick one. (If you immediately know the one thing, you don't need to bother with the list-making process.) Now, envision your future in a two-part drama.

In part one, you have mastered that new habit or behavior and made it part of your life. What does your life look like? How have your surroundings changed? How do you feel? How do people respond to you? What have you gained materially, spiritually, or socially by making this commitment and honoring it? Don't just look at this picture from the outside; immerse yourself in the sights and sounds. Try to put yourself completely into your life as it would be. *Feel* it in your body, *feel* it in your heart, *feel* it in your relationships, *feel* it in your gut.

Part two may not be so much fun, but it is an extremely important part of the process. Envision your life without the new behavior. You did not choose it. Or, you decided to do it but did not follow through. How are others perceiving you? What have you failed to accomplish, how have you failed to grow, because you did not commit and follow through? How do you feel about yourself? What opportunity has been lost? Again, don't be an outside observer and just analyze it intellectually, really feel it. Let your imagination go and envision this dark scenario. Face it. Experience it, and see the tough consequences.

After considering these two realities, make your choice. Commit to doing or not doing it. Tell yourself, this is what I am going to gain if I commit to this course of action, and what I am going to lose if I do not. This is what I stand to gain, this is what I stand to lose. I would suggest going for something really substantial here. For example, if you didn't align your life to your sense of purpose, where would you end up? Or if you continue to dominate interactions with people, what is your life going to look like?

From experience, I know that some people get this right away. Others need to take it home as a practice for a few weeks and pay attention to it before they really feel it in their body, experience it in their relationships, before the consequences of their actions migrate from their heads to their guts. But once it hits home, behavior starts to change. So, if you do not get it right away, I urge you to keep at it for a few weeks. Sticking with it, practicing Building Commitment, can change your life.

> *Be like a postage stamp: stick to one thing until you get there.*
> — Margaret Carty

Aim high with your commitment. Les Brown, a truly inspirational author and speaker whom I admire, once said, "We don't fail because we aim too high and miss; we fail because we aim too low and hit." Building Commitment entails crafting a vision of the future based on an authentic understanding of who we are, where we stand, and where we want to go. It is about creating a vision—positive and negative— about what is at stake. James Collins and Jerry Porras wrote about vision as "knowing 'in your bones' what can or must be done. . . . It isn't forecasting the future, it is creating the future by taking action in the present." *Building Commitment is the path of vision.*

## ACTION MASTERY STEP THREE: BUILDING PRACTICE

Building Practice is the process of consistently engaging in new behaviors to enrich our lives. It is the application phase of growth. While it is crucial to build awareness and to build commitment, they are not sufficient for transformation; consistent action and new, tangible, pragmatic behaviors are required.

Admiring our great insights and feeling proud of our new commitments will not, in themselves, get us to our desired destination. Lao Tzu, who wrote possibly the most profound life and leadership text ever—*Tao Te Ching*—reflected, "A Sage will practice the Tao. A fool will only admire it."

Practice makes potentialities possible. In the January 2005 issue of *Training & Development* magazine, Jack Zenger, Joe Folkman, and Robert Sherwin make an impressive case for Building Practice or what they call "The Promise of Phase 3." In their research, they identified three phases of learning: Phase I, Pre-Session Work; Phase II, Learning Events; Phase III, Follow-Up and Coaching. The results of their study of these three phases were stunning. Organizations typically invested only 10 percent of their resources in Phase I or Prework, 85 percent of their resources in Phase II or Learning Events, and 5 percent in Phase III or Follow-Up and Coaching. Wait a minute. Where was the greatest value gained? In the Phase III follow-up. Think about it. Fifty percent of the value was found to be in Phase III, and most organizations spent only 5 percent of their resources there. Studies by ASTD yielded similarly dramatic results. Learning events followed by coaching culminated in 73 percent better results than training events alone. Coaching is increasingly making the difference between substantial return on investment and minimal return on investment for leadership and learning programs. Recent studies have documented that more than 60 percent of all corporate leadership development programs now include a coaching component.

Building Practice entails devising new, disciplined ways of behaving to enrich our life and the lives of others. Sometimes practices are *inner disciplines* such as meditation, to center ourselves amidst all the dynamic pressures. Another helpful inner discipline is to examine our beliefs from moment to moment, to see if they are opening us up or closing us down. Still another might be to learn to read our physical bodily reactions to gauge our genuine emotional states.

Sometimes practices will be *outer disciplines* like starting the day half an hour earlier for more effective planning; showing more appreciation of employees or family members; listening skills; or exercising on a regular schedule. Whether it is an inner discipline or an *outer* discipline, we have to do it consistently. "To keep the lamp burning," Mother Teresa said, "we have to put oil in it." To keep growing, we have to put practice into it. *Building Practice is the path of discipline.* Discipline bridges us to the benefits, and the benefits generate self-sustaining, continued practice.

When Pablo Casals, whom many consider the greatest cellist ever, was 92 years old, he was practicing five hours a day—more than his best students. One day a frustrated student approached Casals and asked, "Pablo, why are you practicing five hours a day? You are putting your students to shame. Why are you practicing so hard?" Evidently, Pablo responded humbly, "I'm practicing so much because I am FINALLY starting to make progress!" Similarly, after winning the 2008 Buick Invitational at Torrey Pines, *USA Today* reported, Tiger Woods attributed "the best stretch of his career" to hours on the range "tinkering with his swing." Tiger explained, "One of the reasons I made the changes I made is I knew I could attain another level. I'm hitting shots I never could hit before. I'm still getting better." Pablo Casals and Tiger Woods are true masters. Masters measure progress by what they believe is possible, not by what others say about their greatness. Bringing together talent, character, and practice, they create a winning formula for true greatness.

So what is possible for you as a leader? With this vision as a backdrop, commit to your daily plan of practices to elevate your leadership craft to the next level.

Locating a practice or behavior that gives you optimal leverage is step one. But it is crucial to find a practice that stretches you, on the one hand, but also is enjoyable and beneficial enough that you will stick with it, or at the very least return to it later.

Personally, I have to discipline myself to practice people and interpersonal skills with colleagues. I enjoy it when I do it, but it is usually last on my priority list. I naturally gravitate to creating things that make a difference in people's lives. Slowing down to connect when I am compelled to create requires discipline and practice. Sometimes it is really hard, so I have to make it a practice to walk around the office more . . . connecting, listening, telling stories, sharing, and learning what is happening. I remind myself to apply my creativity with people, not only ideas, to keep my strengths, interest, and motivation engaged. If I reframe it as a presence, passion, and idea-generating process, then it connects to my purpose and it has real value to me. When I do it in a manner that is genuine and engaging, morale and energy increase. When I don't, an energy- and morale-depleting cost is levied.

> *We have a "strategic" plan.*
> *It's called doing things.*
> — Herb Kelleher

So, what are the practices and new behaviors that you are going to commit to? Remember, you don't need, or want, 50 things to practice. Not even ten. One or two things, well selected and well practiced, are enough to foster transformation. I recently encountered a top NBA player who had elevated his game to the next level. He was already great, one of the top players in the league. However, his jump shot was just okay, not great. Fortunately, he was aware of this downside and diligently focused his practice on shooting 2,500 jump shots—four to six hours of continuous shooting daily. He did this daily routine seven days a week for nine months. The results: his game became nearly unstoppable. His inside game was more dangerous because he now had an outside game, too.

What do you need to practice 2,500 times per day, or even ten times per day, to take your "game" to the next level? Do you need to strengthen your "inside game" or your "outside game?"

What are you going to practice? Stop. Don't keep reading. Pause. Then, answer the question. What are you going to practice? What new behavior could you practice that would, over time, move you forward? The entire benefit of this book rests on your thoughtful response. Choose well. Stick with it. What you practice, you become.

# REFLECTION
## BUILDING PRACTICE

Review your plans for awareness building and commitment building. Reflect on which specific behaviors or practices would give you the greatest leverage. Get very tangible, specific, and pragmatic here. If most of your development need is in the people arena, then most likely a practice around listening, receiving, and staying open will yield the greatest returns. If your development need is centered around more courageous expression, the practice may be speaking up the next time you feel inhibition, hesitation, or stress in a meeting. Practice speaking up in a way that is consistent with your values and principles. If your development need is about energy and resilience, your practice may be a daily meditation and a fitness program to revive your vitality. Practices at first glance seem small, ordinary, and not too exciting. But over time their benefits accumulate and create a transformative impact. Reflect on and identify the practices that will give you the most leverage to grow.

## THE ART OF COACHING OTHERS

With what we've learned about self-coaching, let's transition to the art of coaching others. Emerson wrote, "We mark with light in the memory the few interviews we have had with

> *It is better to know some of the questions than all of the answers.*
>
> — James Thurber

souls that made our soul wiser, that spoke what we thought, that told us what we know, that gave us leave to be what we inwardly are." Indeed, of all the leadership skills, coaching may be the most important. Why? Helping to foster the growth of those around us gives sustainability to our leadership and perpetuates optimal, ongoing value creation.

*Coaching is the art of drawing forth potential onto the canvas of high performance.* It's the gentle yet firm hand of leadership guiding the way like a caring friend, helping the "coachee" to steer clear of danger or set a more positive course.

Leadership is more than just a job. The leader of a group of any size, from a family, club, congregation, or classroom to a multinational corporation or a nation, sets the tone for all the members of the group. When you are a leader, other people look to you, depend on you. Leaders hold lives and destinies in their hands; this is why leadership can be a sacred calling.

> *You must be the change you wish to see in the world.*
>
> — The Dhammapada

That calling is best honored when the leader sets the highest example of personal and professional behavior, then enlists others to take this challenging path as well. To accomplish both of these tasks, nothing is more vital than coaching. Effective coaching, to bring out the strengths and talents of all the people in the group or organization, serves a dual role. It

is a generous contribution to each individual's growth and fulfillment. At the same time, it is one of the most practical strategies for maximizing the effectiveness and success of the group. The more capable and fully developed each individual in your group, the stronger the group. Each person in the group who is not living up to his or her capabilities is dragging the group down, diminishing its effectiveness. Roger Lacey, Vice President, Corporate Planning & Strategy at 3M Company, shared this perspective on team leadership: "Ultimately, strategy, leadership, and teaming have to find their high-performing intersection. When companies leverage world-class strategy with world-class leadership and teaming, enduring momentum is possible."

For the past several years, LeaderSource has worked with Novartis, a $32-billion global pharmaceutical firm formed in 1997 as a result of a merger between Sandoz and CIBA. Novartis developed a fast-paced and results-oriented culture. By 2001, the company had hired 70 percent of their senior talent on the outside. Fortunately, the "get results" culture also valued coaching and leadership development.

Significant investments were made to assess, develop, coach, and mentor top talent. Dr. Daniel Vasella, Novartis Chairman and CEO, and Thomas Ebeling, CEO of various divisions of Novartis over the past ten years, were substantially supportive and involved in a variety of leadership initiatives. By 2005, only 30 percent of senior talent were hired on the outside. Millions of dollars were saved in recruiting. Millions more were leveraged to produce and sustain results. Thomas Ebeling, one of the best CEO coaches I have ever seen, commented:

> Coaching, leadership development, and mentoring are not tasks you can just delegate to Human Resources. Coaching is one of the most critical leadership skills for optimizing and sustaining individual and team performance. Investing time in coaching and mentoring gives tremendous Return On Investment. It impacts results, retention, morale, and talent identification. . . . Over the course of my career, I've learned that coaching is an extremely valuable and energizing investment. Since I am so results-oriented, it is surprising to people when I tell them that coaching and mentoring has been one of my most satisfying accomplishments.

For many of us, the word *coach* evokes images of a hulking figure in a sweatshirt, blowing a whistle and barking directions to a more or less compliant group of youngsters. But a genuine coach has a far more interesting and refined role than giving orders. If you are on a mountain-climbing expedition, struggling with some difficult terrain, lost in a fog or snowstorm, not able to see the top of the mountain or much of the path ahead, you are grateful for a veteran guide, calling down from above, "Go to the right. Dig in. Watch out for loose rocks. You're doing fine." The guide has perspective, experience that you don't have, and crucial knowledge. Similarly, the players on a sports team, caught up in the moment-to-moment action on the field, have little perspective. An effective coach rises above the playing field to get a more complete picture from which to call the plays and direct the action.

Some coaches simply assert their expertise. Great coaches blend expertise and facilitation to help the players go beyond their previously held boundaries. In his book *Masterful Coaching*, Robert Hargrove notes, "When most people think of learning they don't think in terms of having to change themselves. They tend to think of learning as . . . acquiring ideas, tips, techniques, and so on. Seldom does it occur to them that the problems they are facing are inseparable from who they are or the way they think and interact with other people." Coaching helps us to step back to see more of the whole person and more of the whole situation, as well as the dynamics between the two.

A senior team for a global company was struggling. They led the North American operations, which was responsible for 40 percent of the global revenue of the high-technology firm. Sales and profits were flat. The pace of new initiatives was slowing. Energy and morale were deteriorating. The new CEO, full of energy, drive, and strong people skills, was hitting the wall after only four months. Why? The dysfunctional relationships of five key team members was paralyzing the effectiveness of a team of 20. The problem? All five of the

> *Life is a series of collisions with the future; it is not a sum of what we have seen but what we yearn to be.*
> — José Ortega y Gassett

difficult people were highly competitive, bright, and valued in their respective functions. The easy solution, firing all five, wasn't so easy. All five team members thought they were right and the rest of the team were "impossible to work with" and "not trustworthy." While meetings were full of conflict and avoidance, team members' off-line comments about one another were toxic.

The typical event-driven team-building process would not get to these core dynamics. Instead, we initiated deep, intensive work with each individual. It was imperative that team members each sort out their issues and take personal responsibility. Only then could we begin having authentic conversations and initiate coaching on their interpersonal dynamics. With progress in these areas, we began a larger teaming initiative. In addition, the CEO needed to step in and make some tough calls to transition two people. Over a six-to-nine-month period, the team re-engaged, sales and profit were regained, and morale returned. Transformation is not an event but a challenging process of working through the coaching needs of leaders, teams, and organizations simultaneously.

Athletes have coaches. Actors have coaches. Politicians have coaches. Increasingly, business people have coaches. Too often, business coaches aim for a charm-school or image-enhancement outcome. That is not enough. We need to develop a new lineage of coaches who focus on transformation leading to exceptional, sustainable performance, whose aim is developing the whole person rather than merely tweaking the external facade. To accomplish this, coaches need to move from an expert or fix-it model concerned primarily with competencies, learning skills, and techniques to a transformative model focused on fundamentally shifting people's view about themselves, their values, and their sense of purpose. Then, coaches need to help people to apply new skills and behaviors.

Influenced by the work of Hargrove, most coaching today fits within one of five categories:

- Expert Coaching: building skills, competencies, and knowledge;
- Pattern Coaching: revealing old patterns and building new patterns of belief and behavior;
- Transformative Coaching: fostering a fundamental shift in point of view, values, and identity;
- Transcendent Coaching: comprehending purpose;
- Integrative Coaching: blending the depth of personal (inside-out) work with the complexity of external (outside-in) dynamics around team, organizational, marketplace, and societal needs.

Most internal coaching programs in organizations deal with Expert Coaching, and many refer to this type of coaching as mentoring. Many external coaches begin and end their level of impact here, as well. Most external coaching resources deal with Expert and Pattern Coaching. An increasing number of coaches do Transformative Coaching, but fewer engage in Transcendent or Integrative Coaching. Ideally, as the coaching industry matures, more world-class, enterprise coaches will emerge who are adept at all five levels and can apply them flexibly to the particular needs of leaders, teams, and organizations.

## COACHING OTHERS TO BUILD AWARENESS

As leaders, we are constantly faced with the task of Building Awareness. Awareness of changing market conditions, emerging economic realities, new capital needs, cost concerns, and operational issues dominates our time and attention. But often the greatest task of Building Awareness is in the human, interpersonal domain. I would venture to say that 70 percent of business problems today are of a human, interpersonal nature. People problems are typically quite complex, yet when individuals, teams, or managers in conflict come to us with their concerns, don't we easily slip into a reactive, knee-jerk mode, look for a simple fix?

Helping others to Build Awareness requires discipline on the part of the coach to stay out of the expert or fix-it approaches to coaching. If we don't, the awareness we build will be only our own awareness. We will be imposing our awareness onto the coachee instead of building the coachee's awareness from the inside-out. St. Theresa of Lisieux explained it this way: "One of the most difficult things about being a spiritual director is to encourage people along paths you would not choose for yourself." Building Awareness requires openness to help those we are coaching to sort out their current reality for themselves and begin to chart out alternative future possibilities.

## BUILDING AWARENESS IN OTHERS

To guide your ability to Build Awareness with people you coach, keep the following principles in mind:

- *Stay open and bring clarity.* Most "answers" lie within the person, the team, and the organization; your job is to help to clarify and reveal them.

> *Just be what you are and speak from your guts and heart—it's all a man has.*
> — Hubert Humphrey

- *Use questions to help the person sort out the current situation.* Before we can move forward with power, we need to know where we stand, understanding both life-enriching and life-damaging behavior and beliefs. "I've found that I can only change how I act if I stay aware of my beliefs and assumptions," writes Margaret Wheatley, author of *Leadership and the New Science.* Very few people take the time, or possess the necessary introspective skills, to do this without the gentle prodding of a coach. Keep in mind the Native American saying, "The first people had questions and they were free. The second people had answers and they were forever enslaved." *Questions are the language of coaching.* They are powerful tools for transformation because, as Bertrand Russell taught, "In all affairs it's a healthy thing now and then to hang a question mark on things you have long taken for granted."

- *Be courageous.* As Robert Hargrove advises, "Be courageous enough to discuss the undiscussable." The coach's job is to shed light on dark regions previously unexplored.

- *Practice speaking directly but with caring.* Help coachees compassionately to see their limitations as well as their gifts. Keep in mind: directness without caring will create resistance, while directness with compassion will create openness. Confront in a caring manner.

- *Help coachees to explore the differences between their intentions and other people's perceptions.* Discrepancies between how people see themselves vs. how others perceive them often hold the key to new self-knowledge and overcoming blind spots. Helping people to see aspects of themselves through the eyes of others can be challenging, but effective. Use 360° feedback tools and merge them with Personal Mastery work to create a 720° (inside-out/outside-in) process.

- *Build Awareness by example.* The greatest teachers and coaches teach as much by their being as by their doing. If you strive for authenticity, open up to your strengths and deficiencies, align with your life-purpose, and serve other people, you will consistently create more value in everything you do. Those you coach will model their lives upon what you are living. *The Bhagavad-Gita*, an invaluable ancient handbook on leadership development, guides us: "Whatsoever a great man does, the very same is also done by other men. Whatever standard he sets, the world follows it." Or as Anne Sophie Swetchine so beautifully put it, "There is a transcendent power in example. We reform others unconsciously when we walk uprightly."

- *Help people to uncover and align with what is meaningful and important to them.* As coachees discover the core principles which guide their meaningful contributions in the world, help them to explore how aligned or misaligned the various parts of their lives (i.e., personal, family, community, career, spiritual) are with these values. An effective transformational coach is both an archeologist who helps to unearth the important structures—that is, the core meaningful contributions—supporting our past, and an architect, who helps us construct a future more aligned with these principles and values.

## COACHING OTHERS TO BUILD COMMITMENT

To elicit commitment, we must help people to envision the positive and negative outcomes—what they will gain and what they will lose—if they continue on their current path. When the emotions deeply register both the compelling reasons to change and the damaging behaviors to leave behind, transformation begins. In the words of Margaret Wheatley, "The greatest source of courage is to realize that if we don't act, nothing will change for the better."

To guide your ability to Build Commitment with people you coach, keep the following principles in mind:

- *Help People to Sort Out Consequences.* By guiding people to grasp the life-enriching and life-damaging consequences of their current behavior or path, you help them to feel the creative tension between where they want to end up and where they are actually headed as a result of their actions. Helping people to envision these alternative futures and to make new life choices is the essence of building commitment. Remember, the person has to see and feel these consequences for himself or herself, not just see your version of the consequences.
- *Allow Your Commitment to Catalyze Their Commitment.* Often it is the emotional engagement of the coach that serves as the impetus for the transformation to begin. "There comes that mysterious meeting in life when someone acknowledges who we are and what we can be, igniting the circuits of our highest potential," writes Rusty Berkus.

> *To find yourself, think for yourself.*
>
> — Socrates

- *Look for Openings.* Commitment is far more likely to take place when vulnerability is sufficiently high. Look for these openings and leverage their growth potential. Situations that might make people more open to commitment include less than positive performance reviews, tough 360° feedback, life traumas, career setbacks, relational breakdowns, broken commitments by others, new or exceptional challenges, need for new skills, lack of preparedness, fear of failure, and new career or life responsibilities. Look for these openings as an opportunity to accelerate progress.
- *Make Sure Commitment Leads to Practice.* Commitment without practice is like an explorer who reviews expedition maps but never leaves home. If commitment does not lead to practice, then it is your responsibility as the coach to help the coachee do one of two things: (1) Explore more deeply the consequences of staying on his or her current track, in order to achieve a more genuine emotional engagement leading to actual practice; (2) Find new practices that are more suited to the person. Not everything works for everyone.
- *Be Patient.* As coaches we are motivated to help people grow now. However, as leaders we each need to unfold at our own pace. If you must be impatient, be impatient with developing your own enhanced skills as a coach.

- *Remember the Why*. Coaches remind people what is at stake and why they are doing something in the first place. Use the "Power of Why" to uncover the person's underlying fears, assumptions, beliefs, and motivators. Wait for the right moment of opening to ask in a caring manner, "Why?" If one "Why?" doesn't get to the heart of things, you may ask two or three times in a row in order to dive deeply under the surface conversation. Ancient sages say five "Whys" will usually get you to the essence of everything.

## COACHING OTHERS TO BUILD PRACTICE

Building Practice is the third stage of transformational coaching. Without practice, there is no transformation. Practice breathes life into our new awareness and commitment. We can be fully aware and committed to noble goals, but if we fail to practice them, it is like someone who lights a lamp and then closes his eyes. "In the end," said Max De Pree, "it is important to remember that we cannot become what we need to be by remaining where we were."

A while ago a somewhat skeptical new coaching client came to me with his most recent 360° assessment and a knowing "I told you so" look on his face. When I asked him, "Why the peculiar look?" he said, "I've had the same 360° assessment for the past five years. Every time, the same results! What a worthless process!" I tried to explore with him the specifics of what he actually practiced as part of the process. It was no surprise to find out he practiced nothing. You know the moral of that story: Nothing practiced, nothing gained.

Beginning practice makes the possible probable; advanced, enduring practice makes the possible real. Practices involve the consistent repetition of new behaviors that transform our lives. Exercise is a practice to build health. Meditation is a practice to unfold our spiritual life. Reflecting at the end of each day on how our interpersonal interactions went is a practice that builds relational effectiveness. Not letting fears or limiting beliefs sabotage our goals can be a lifelong practice for most of us, helping us to move forward when the easier path would be to remain where we are, locked in our limiting belief systems.

For a practice to become a habit, often it needs to be consistently engaged for at least 40 days. A day here and a day there will not effect transformation. At first our practice requires discipline, that is, doing something we may not be inclined to do. Over time, however, the discipline is replaced by the life-enriching benefits we are gaining; then the practice becomes more self-sustaining and requires less effort. If we "fall off the wagon" of our practice, so to speak, we want to get back on to regain the benefits.

To guide your ability to Build Practice with people you coach, keep the following principles in mind:

- *Co-Create the Practice with the Person.*

  A practice must push boundaries but also be suitable to the person. Ask the person you are coaching, "What new behavior could you practice that over time would move you forward?" Then, take time to brainstorm together to co-create a meaningful practice. Keep the practices simple and defined. Make sure the person wants to give the practice a try.

- *Hold the Person Accountable.*

  Define how often the person will do the practice (daily, twice a day, etc.) and over what duration (a week, a month, etc.). Meet with the person to audit progress and lack of progress. Hold the person accountable, set new goals, and create new practices, as needed.

- *Avoid Intellectualizing.*

  Thinking about doing something is not the same as doing something. So make sure your practices are behaviors that engage the person in a new way vs. only thinking about behaving in a new way but never actually taking the leap into action.

- *Just Do It . . . or Do Something Else.*

  While some practices are more dynamic (exercise, asserting our viewpoint, expressing our values) and others are more reflective (pausing to center ourselves, reflecting on our day), the key to practice is taking action. An initial practice may not be the one that revolutionizes the person's life, but it is the beginning of a process that will lead to a practice that does have an impact. Sometimes the most important contribution a coach can make is to keep people trying new practices and then helping them struggle through the challenges that come up until they settle on an enduring practice and improvement takes place.

> *"Come to the edge," he said.*
> *They said, "We are afraid."*
> *"Come to the edge," he said.*
> *They came. He pushed*
> *them, . . . and they flew.*
> — Guillaume Appollinaire

Commit yourself to the process of building awareness, commitment, and practice, as well as to coaching yourself and all those you touch in your life. The results will be life changing.

## PARTING THOUGHTS FOR YOUR JOURNEY AHEAD

After years of coaching leaders behind closed doors, I find it both a challenge and a joy to take the time to share these principles with you. David Bohm once wrote, "The ability to perceive or think differently is more important than the knowledge gained." In this spirit, I hope this book has been more than just an interesting intellectual excursion that leads to a "smart book" gathering dust on a "smart bookcase." I hope it has been a thought-provoking journey for you. I also hope you have grown a little since you first opened the cover. But my real hope is that over time you will make the commitment to integrate the key principles shared and breathe them into your life. I hope each day you will take slightly "deeper breaths" until the inspiration is fully yours.

A friend shared a small story from the *Talmud* that tells the whole story of life and leadership: "Every blade of grass in all of creation has an angel bent over it whispering three words of encouragement: Grow . . . Grow . . . Grow." That's my wish for you: grow in authenticity, grow in influence, grow in value creation.

# THE JOURNEY CONTINUES

Ten years have passed since I finished writing the first edition of this book. As it is with most things, "being away" for a while can bring a fresh, objective perspective. Reflecting on the book, I started to think, "What is the real purpose of this book?" I don't mean just the words or concepts, but its true potential contribution. What value can it potentially serve?

Certainly the principal purpose of *Leadership from the Inside Out* is to give people tools for personal growth and transformation leading to leadership growth and transformation. But its true potential contribution is more than that. Its purpose is more than just helping a bunch of separate individuals to grow.

Imagine a critical mass of authentic leaders who express their gifts and create life-enriching value. Imagine an organization like that, or a community, or a family. Envisioning a better world seems less like an idealized fantasy when you think what a critical mass of authentic leaders could achieve. As you move forward, I challenge you not to get lost in your own growth—the purpose of your transformation is to radiate your gifts in the service of others. Growth is much more meaningful when it touches and enriches the lives of others.

Quite some time ago, I was working with a CEO known for his exceptional visionary skills and performance results. Throughout his career he had always been ahead of the strategic curve. He had an innate sense for what was "next" long before his peers or competitors. His long track record of breakthrough product introductions and marketplace successes was testimony to his exceptional gifts.

In his coaching sessions we focused on continuing to leverage his strategic excellence while helping him find more balance in his life. After about six months of coaching, global marketplace conditions had dramatically shifted and his company found itself in an extremely vulnerable position. For the first time in his career, he had missed a major strategic initiative. He could easily have diverted blame to many other people. Fortunately he did not. He faced the troops and took full, ultimate responsibility for the strategic oversight. He asked everyone for their support in moving forward. His authenticity, emotional courage, and self-esteem were strong enough for him to take genuine responsibility. As you would expect, morale skyrocketed, corporate energy was refocused, and the company emerged even stronger.

As powerful as one authentic leader can be for an organization, a critical mass of leaders growing from the inside-out can greatly accelerate organizational progress. The chairman and CEO of a firm invited me out to breakfast to discuss a new coaching candidate. When

> *The only way to discover the limits of the possible is to go beyond them into the impossible.*
>
> — Arthur C. Clarke

I arrived at the restaurant, I was surprised to be greeted by the entire executive management team minus the coaching candidate. In our meeting, we focused on the "issues" of their fellow executive and how each member of the team perceived what he needed to improve. After listening to their concerns, I was confident that we could help the individual, but that was not the real issue. Expressing what I sensed was the actual organizational need, I challenged the team, "What are each of you doing to grow as leaders in order to grow your organization?" In spite of their extremely aggressive business plans, no one could respond to my question. Clarifying my question, I said, "We can help Fred, but the real organizational issue is not to improve Fred's performance. The real issue is: How are you preparing yourselves for success?"

Leaving the meeting, I felt that although I had isolated their real needs, I had likely lost a potential account. Two days later, however, the chairman and CEO called me and said, "We listened to your counsel and felt you were right on target. I would like to discuss how all the members of our senior team, including me, could engage in coaching along with Fred." Within four months, the entire senior team was deeply involved in coaching. A critical mass of individuals was now rapidly transforming the organization. The chairman was now ready to let go of the CEO responsibilities. Since the members of the senior team did not want the CEO job, an external search was initiated. Key members of the team began to transform their roles, and new positions were created that energized the company and addressed strategic issues. A common language about growth and transformation permeated the organization. A new culture, one that would support growth and transformation, was now on its way. Like this company, organizations that invest as proactively in people development as they do in business development will thrive for decades to come.

I hope you will continue the journey we have started. I also hope you will share your blessings with others—share them with your organization, with your customers, and with your loved ones. Together we can begin to create a better world.

*Until one is committed there is hesitancy, the chance to draw back, always ineffectiveness. . . . Boldness has genius, power, and magic in it. Begin it now.*

— Goethe

# NOTES

## CHAPTER ONE: PERSONAL MASTERY

Page 33   Youth Frontiers is a nonpartisan, nonprofit organization dedicated to improving school climate by building character through teaching students to incorporate kindness, courage, respect, leadership, and wisdom into their daily lives.

Page 35   M. M. Lombardo and R. W. Eichinger, *Top Ten Career Stallers and Stoppers, The Leadership Architect: Norms and Validity Report* (4th ed.) (Minneapolis: Lominger International, A Korn/Ferry Company, 2003).

Page 35   Kenneth R. Brousseau, Michael J. Driver, Gary Hourihan, and Rikard Larsson, "The Seasoned Executive's Decision-Making Style," *Harvard Business Review* (February 2006): 111–121.

Page 35   Daniel J. Siegel, *The Developing Mind: How Relationships and the Brain Interact to Shape Who We Are* (New York: Guilford Press, 1999), 2–3.

Page 37   Jim Collins, *Good to Great: Why Some Companies Make the Leap . . . and Others Don't* (New York: HarperCollins, 2001), 27–30.

Page 37   Jim Collins, *Good to Great*, 25–40.

Page 37   Daniel Goleman, *Working with Emotional Intelligence* (New York: Bantam, 1998), 26–27.

Page 37   Daniel Goleman, Richard Boyatzis, and Annie McKee, *Primal Leadership: Learning to Lead with Emotional Intelligence* (Boston: Harvard Business School Press, 2004), 94.

Page 44   Howard Schultz and Dori Jones Yang, *Pour Your Heart into It: How Starbucks Built a Company One Cup at a Time* (New York: Hyperion, 1997), 147–152.

Page 48   Kenneth R. Brousseau et al., "The Seasoned Executive's Decision-Making Style," 111–121.

Page 55   John Passmore, "An Integrative Executive Coaching Model," *Consulting Psychology Journal: Practice and Research* (March 2007): 68–78.

Page 57   *Business Week*, August 2007.

## CHAPTER TWO: PURPOSE MASTERY

Page 62   Mihaly Csikszentmihalyi, *Flow: The Psychology of Optimal Experience* (New York: Harper-Perrenial, 1991), 43–70.

Page 63  Martin E. P. Seligman, *Authentic Happiness: Using the New Positive Psychology to Realize Your Potential for Lasting Fulfillment* (New York: Free Press, 2004), 166.

Page 65  Nikos Mourkogiannis, *Purpose: The Starting Point of Great Companies* (New York: Palgrave Macmillan, 2006), 114.

Page 72  Mihaly Csikszentmihalyi, *Flow: The Psychology of Optimal Experience*, 69.

Page 72  Michael M. Lombardo and Robert W. Eichinger, *FYI, For Your Improvement: A Guide for Development and Coaching* (Minneapolis: Lominger Limited, 2004), 386.

Page 72  Jim Collins, *Good to Great*, 193–197.

Page 73  Howard Schultz and Dori Jones Yang, *Pour Your Heart into It*, 81.

## CHAPTER THREE: INTERPERSONAL MASTERY

Page 79  John H. Zenger and Joseph Folkman, *The Extraordinary Leader: Turning Good Managers into Great Leaders* (New York: McGraw-Hill, 2002), 149–150.

Page 83  Leigh Branham and Saratoga Institute, *The 7 Hidden Reasons Employees Leave: How to Recognize the Subtle Signs and Act before It's Too Late* (New York: American Management Association, 2005).

Page 86  Peter Senge, C. Otto Scharmer, Joseph Jaworski, and Betty Sue Flowers, *Presence: An Exploration of Profound Change in People, Organizations, and Society* (New York: Doubleday Currency, 2005), 141.

Page 90  Robert W. Eichinger, Michael M. Lombardo, and Dave Ulrich, *100 Things You Need to Know: Best People Practices for Managers & HR* (Minneapolis: Lominger Limited, 2006), 193.

## CHAPTER FOUR: CHANGE MASTERY

Page 107  These insights extracted from a discussion about Change Mastery in January 2008.

Page 107  Center for Creative Leadership research presented at Conference Board Executive Coaching Conference, February 2008.

Page 107  M. M. Lombardo and R. W. Eichinger, *The Leadership Machine*, researched by Lominger International (Minneapolis: Lominger International, 2001).

Page 107  Center for Creative Leadership research presented at Conference Board Executive Coaching Conference, February 2008.

Page 108  M. M. Lombardo and R. W. Eichinger, *Preventing Derailment: What to Do Before It's Too Late* (Greensboro, NC: Center for Creative Leadership, 1989); M. M. Lombardo and R. W.

Eichinger, "High Potentials as High Learners," *Human Resource Management* (2000): 39, 321–329; R. J. Sternberg, R. K. Wagner, W. M. Williams, and J. A. Horvath, "Testing Common Sense," *American Psychologist* (1995): 50, 912–927; Daniel Goleman, *Emotional Intelligence* (New York: Bantam Books, 1995).

Page 108  M. M. Lombardo and R. W. Eichinger, *FYI for Your Improvement.* (Minneapolis: Lominger Limited, 2004).

Page 109  M. M. Lombardo and R. W. Eichinger, "High Potentials as High Learners," 39, 321–329; A. H. Church and E. I. Derosiers, *Talent Management: Will the High Potentials Please Stand Up?* (symposium presented at the Society for Industrial and Organizational Psychology Conference, Dallas, 2006); J. A. Connolly and C. Viswesvaran, "Assessing the Construct Validity of a Measure of Learning Agility" (presentation at the Seventeenth Annual Conference of the Society for Industrial and Organizational Psychology, Toronto, Canada, April 2002).

Page 117  Research by Lominger International.

Page 118  David Rock and Jeffrey Schwartz, "The Neuroscience of Leadership," *Strategy+Business* (Summer 2006).

## CHAPTER FIVE: RESILIENCE MASTERY

Page 129  Jody Miller, "Get a Life," *Fortune*, November 28, 2005, http://www.CNNMoney.com.

Page 130  Tony Schwartz and Catherine McCarthy, "Manage Your Energy, Not Your Time," *Harvard Business Review* (October 2007).

Page 136  James Loehr, Ed.D., and Jack Groppel, Ph.D., "Stress & Recovery: Important Keys to Engagement," *Chief Learning Officer Magazine*, October 2004.

Page 138  John Douillard, *Body, Mind & Sport: The Mind-Body Guide to Lifelong Fitness & Your Personal Best* (New York: Crown Publishing, 1995).

Page 141  Daniel H. Pink, *A Whole New Mind: Moving from the Information Age to the Conceptual Age* (New York: Penguin, 2005), 177–197.

## CHAPTER SIX: BEING MASTERY

Page 147  Jon Kabat-Zinn, *Wherever You Go There You Are: Mindfulness Meditation in Everyday Life* (New York: Hyperion, 1994), 4–5.

Page 148  Maharishi Mahesh Yogi, founder of Transcendental Meditation.

Page 149 David Rock and Jeffrey Schwartz, "Why Neuroscience Matters to Executives," *Strategy+Business*, Online Event, November 2, 2006.

Page 150  David Rock and Jeffrey Schwartz, "Why Neuroscience Matters to Executives."

Page 150  Peter Senge, C. Otto Scharmer, Joseph Jaworski, and Betty Sue Flowers, *Presence: An Exploration of Profound Change in People, Organizations, and Society* (New York: Doubleday Currency, 2005), 85–91.

Page 151 David Rock and Jeffrey Schwartz, "The Neuroscience of Leadership," *Strategy+Business* (Summer 2006).

Page 151  These insights extracted from a discussion on Being Mastery.

Page 151 Anne Fisher, "Be Smarter at Work, Slack Off," *Fortune,* March 17, 2006, http://www .CNNMoney.com,

Page 155 Transcendental Meditation research; Sharon Begley, "What the Beatles Gave Science," *Newsweek*, November 2007.

Page 155 Jon Kabat-Zinn, *Full Catastrophe Living: Using the Wisdom of Your Body and Mind to Face Stress, Pain, and Illness* (New York: Bantam Dell, 2005); University of Massachusetts: Center for Mindfulness research; Joel Stein, "Just Say Om," *Time,* http://www.time.com:/time/magazine/article0,9171, 4171136,00; Daniel Goleman, "Finding Happiness: Cajole Your Brain to Lean to the Left," *New York Times*, February 4, 2003.

Page 156  David Rock and Jeffrey Schwartz, "Why Neuroscience Matters to Executives."

## CHAPTER SEVEN: ACTION MASTERY

Page 167 Sharon Begley, *Train Your Mind, Change Your Brain: How a New Science Reveals Our Extraordinary Potential to Transform Ourselves* (New York: Ballantine, 2007), 241.

Page 170 Malcolm Gladwell, *Blink: The Power of Thinking without Thinking* (New York: Little, Brown, 2005).

Page 170  Daniel Goleman, *Working with Emotional Intelligence* (New York: Bantam, 1998), 67.

Page 171  Noel Tichy and Warren Bennis, *Wise Leaders Cultivate Two Traits: Leadership Excellence* 24 (June 2007): 3.

Page 175  Jack Zenger, Joe Folkman, and Robert Sherwin, "The Promise of Phase 3," *Training and Development* (January 2005): 31–34.

Page 175  American Society for Training and Development (ASTD) research.

Page 176  Steve DiMeglio, "Woods Makes Statement, Wins Buick Invitational," *USA Today*, January 2008.

Page 179  Robert Hargrove, *Masterful Coaching: Extraordinary Results by Impacting People and the Way They Think and Work Together* (San Francisco: Jossey-Bass, 1995), 27.

# BIBLIOGRAPHY

*The following is a combined list of resources used and
recommended readings:*

Arbinger Institute. *Leadership and Self-Deception: Getting Out of the Box.* San Francisco: Berrett-Koehler, 2002.

Arenander, Alarik T., and Craig Pearson. *Upgrading the Executive Brain: Breakthrough Science and Technology of Leadership.* www.theleadersbrain.org.

Begley, Sharon. *Train Your Mind, Change Your Brain: How a New Science Reveals Our Extraordinary Potential to Transform Ourselves.* New York: Ballantine, 2007.

Bennis, Warren. *On Becoming a Leader.* Reading, MA: Addison-Wesley, 1990.

Bennis, Warren, and Patricia Ward Biederman. *Organizing Genius: The Secrets of Creative Collaboration.* Reading, MA: Addison-Wesley, 1996.

Bennis, Warren, and Burt Nanus. *Leaders: The Strategies for Taking Charge.* New York: Harper Business, 1985.

Bennis, Warren, and Robert J. Thomas. *Leading for a Lifetime: How Defining Moments Shape Leaders of Today and Tomorrow.* Cambridge, MA: Harvard Business School Press, 2007.

Block, Peter. *Stewardship: Choosing Service over Self-Interest.* San Francisco: Berrett-Koehler, 1996.

Bolman, Lee, and Terrence E. Deal. *Leading with Soul: An Uncommon Journey to Spirit.* San Francisco: Jossey-Bass, 1994.

Boyatzis, Richard E., and Annie McKee. *Resonant Leadership: Renewing Yourself and Connecting with Others through Mindfulness, Hope and Compassion.* Cambridge, MA: Harvard Business School Press, 2005.

Branden, Nathaniel. *Six Pillars of Self-Esteem.* New York: Bantam Books, 1995.

Bridges, William. *Transitions: Making Sense of Life's Changes.* Reading, MA: Addison-Wesley, 1980.

Brousseau, Kenneth R., Michael J. Driver, Gary Hourihan, and Rikard Larsson. "The Seasoned Executive's Decision-Making Style," *Harvard Business Review* (February 2006): 111–121.

Byron, Thomas. *Dhammapada: The Sayings of the Buddha*. Boston: Shambhala, 1976.

Campbell, Joseph. *The Power of Myth*. New York: Doubleday, 1988.

Carter, Jimmy. *Beyond the White House: Waging Peace, Fighting Disease, Building Hope*. New York: Simon & Schuster, 2007.

Cashman, Kevin, with Jack Forem. *Awakening the Leader Within: A Story of Transformation*. Hoboken, NJ: John Wiley & Sons, 2003.

Cavanaugh, Joseph. *Respectfully, Joe Cavanaugh* [video]. St. Paul, MN: Kelley Productions and Twin Cities Public Television, 1994.

Charan, Ram, Stephen Drotter, and James Noel. *The Leadership Pipeline: How to Build the Leadership Powered Company*. San Francisco: Jossey-Bass, 2001.

Chouinard, Yvon. *Let My People Go Surfing: The Education of a Reluctant Businessman*. New York: Penguin, 2005.

Collins, Jim. *Good to Great: Why Some Companies Make the Leap . . . and Others Don't*. New York: HarperCollins, 2001.

Costa, John Dalla. *The Ethical Imperative: Why Moral Leadership Is Good Business*. Cambridge, MA: Perseus, 1998.

Covey, Stephen R. *The 7 Habits of Highly Effective People*. New York: Simon & Schuster, 1990.

Csikszentmihalyi, Mihaly. *Flow: The Psychology of Optimal Experience*. New York: Harper Perennial, 1991.

DeFoore, Bill, and John Renesch, eds. *The New Bottom Line: Bringing Heart and Soul to Business*. San Francisco: New Leaders Press, 1996.

Dotlich, David, Ph.D., Peter Cairo, Ph.D., and Stephen Rhinesmith, Ph.D. *Head, Heart and Guts: How the World's Best Companies Develop Leaders*. San Francisco: Jossey-Bass, 2006.

Douillard, John. *Body, Mind & Sport: The Mind-Body Guide to Lifelong Fitness & Your Personal Best*. New York: Crown Publishing, 1995.

Driver, Michael J., Ken R. Brousseau, and Phillip Hunsaker. *The Dynamic Decision Maker: Five Decision Styles for Executive and Business Success*. New York: Excel, 1998.

Eichinger, Robert W., Michael M. Lombardo, and Dave Ulrich. *100 Things You Need to Know: Best People Practices for Managers & HR*. Minneapolis: Lominger Limited, 2006.

Einstein, Albert. *Einstein on Humanism: Collected Essays of Albert Einstein*. Secaucus, NJ: Carol Publishing, 1993.

Emerson, Ralph Waldo. *The Collected Works of Ralph Waldo Emerson*. Cambridge, MA: Belknap, 1984.

Garfield, Charles. *Peak Performance*. New York: Warner Books, 1989.

George, Bill, with Peter Sims. *True North: Discover Your Authentic Leadership*. San Francisco: Jossey-Bass, 2007.

Gladwell, Malcolm. *Blink: The Power of Thinking without Thinking*. New York: Little, Brown, 2005.

Goleman, Daniel. *Emotional Intelligence: Why It Can Matter More Than IQ*. New York: Bantam, 1994.

Goleman, Daniel. *Social Intelligence: The New Science of Human Relationships*. New York: Bantam, 2006.

Goleman, Daniel. *Working with Emotional Intelligence*. New York: Bantam, 1998.

Goleman, Daniel, Richard Boyatzis, and Annie McKee. *Primal Leadership: Learning to Lead with Emotional Intelligence*. Boston: Harvard Business School Press, 2004.

Goss, Tracy. *The Last Word on Power: Executive Re-invention for Leaders Who Must Make the Impossible Happen*. New York: Bantam Doubleday Dell, 1996.

Greenleaf, Robert K. *Servant Leadership: A Journey into the Nature of Legitimate Power and Greatness*. Mahwah, NJ: Paulist Press, 1977.

Groppel, Jack L., and Bob Andelman. *The Corporate Athlete: How to Achieve Maximal Performance in Business and Life*. New York: John Wiley & Sons, 1999.

Halpern, Belle Linda, and Kathy Lubar. *Leadership Presence: Dramatic Techniques to Reach Out, Motivate and Inspire*. New York: Gotham Books, 2004.

Hargrove, Robert. *Masterful Coaching: Extraordinary Results by Impacting People and the Way They Think and Work Together*. San Francisco: Jossey-Bass, 1995.

Hawley, John A. *Reawakening the Spirit in Work*. New York: Simon & Schuster, 1995.

Heider, Joseph. *Tao of Leadership*. New York: Bantam Books, 1986.

Hendricks, Gay, and Kate Ludeman. *The Corporate Mystic: A Guidebook for Visionaries with Their Feet on the Ground*. New York: Bantam Books, 1996.

Hillman, James. *The Soul's Code: In Search of Character and Calling.* New York: Random House, 1996.

Jaworski, Joseph. *Synchronicity: The Inner Path of Leadership.* San Francisco: Berrett-Koehler, 1996.

Jung, C. G. *Basic Writings of C. G. Jung.* New York: Random House, 1993.

Kabat-Zinn, Jon. *Coming to Our Senses: Healing Ourselves and the World through Mindfulness.* New York: Hyperion, 2005.

Kabat-Zinn, Jon. *Full Catastrophe Living: Using the Wisdom of Your Body and Mind to Face Stress, Pain, and Illness.* New York: Bantam Dell, 2005.

Kabat-Zinn, Jon. *Wherever You Go There You Are: Mindfulness Meditation in Everyday Life.* New York: Hyperion, 1994.

Kets DeVries, Manfred. *Leaders, Fools and Imposters: Essays on the Psychology of Leadership.* San Francisco: Jossey-Bass, 1993.

Kouzes, James M., and Barry Z. Posner. *The Leadership Challenge.* San Francisco: Jossey-Bass, 2007.

Leider, Richard. *The Power of Purpose: Creating Meaning in Your Life and Work.* San Francisco: Berrett-Koehler, 2005.

Loehr, Jim, and Tony Schwartz. *The Power of Full Engagement: Managing Energy, Not Time, Is the Key to High Performance and Personal Renewal.* New York: Simon & Schuster, 2003.

Lombardo, Michael M., and Robert W. Eichinger. *FYI, For Your Improvement: A Guide for Development and Coaching.* Minneapolis: Lominger Limited, 2004.

Lowen, Alexander. *Narcissism: Denial of the True Self.* New York: Collier Books, 1995.

Maharishi Mahesh Yogi. *Bhagavad-Gita: A New Translation and Commentary.* Fairfield, CA: Age of Enlightenment Press, 1967.

Maslow, Abraham. *Toward a Psychology of Being.* New York: Van Nostrand-Rheinhold, 1968.

Melrose, Ken. *Making the Grass Greener on Your Side.* San Francisco: Berrett-Koehler, 1995.

Merton, Thomas. *No Man Is an Island.* New York: Walker, 1986.

Morris, Tom. *True Success: A New Philosophy of Excellence.* New York: Putnam, 1994.

Mourkogiannis, Nikos. *Purpose: The Starting Point of Great Companies.* New York: Palgrave Macmillan, 2006.

O'Neil, John. *Success and Your Shadow*. Boulder, CO: Sounds True Audio, 1995.

Osbourn, Carol. *Inner Excellence: Spiritual Principles of Life Driven Business*. San Rafael, CA: New World Library, 1992.

Parry, Danaan. *Warriors of the Heart*. Bainbridge Island, WA: Earthstewards Network, 1997.

Patnaude, Jeff. *Leading from the Maze: A Personal Pathway to Leadership*. Berkeley, CA: Ten Speed Press, 1996.

Pearman, Roger R., Michael M. Lombardo, and Robert W. Eichinger. *You: Being More Effective in Your MBTI Type*. Minneapolis: Lominger Limited, 2005.

Pink, Daniel H. *A Whole New Mind: Moving from the Information Age to the Conceptual Age*. New York: Penguin, 2005.

Rechtschaffen, Stephan. *Time Shifting: Creating More Time to Enjoy Your Life*. New York: Doubleday Currency, 1996.

Rock, David. *Quiet Leadership: Six Steps to Transforming Performance at Work*. New York: Harper-Collins, 2006.

Scharmer, Otto C. *Theory U: Leading from the Future as It Emerges*. Cambridge, MA: Society for Organizational Learning, 2007.

Schneider, Bruce D. *Energy Leadership: Transforming Your Workplace and Your Life*. Hoboken, NJ: John Wiley & Sons, 2007.

Schultz, Howard, and Dori Jones Yang. *Pour Your Heart into It: How Starbucks Built a Company One Cup at a Time*. New York: Hyperion, 1997.

Schwartz, Tony, and Catherine McCarthy. "Manage Your Energy, Not Your Time," *Harvard Business Review* (October 2007).

Segal, Jeanne. *Raising Your Emotional Intelligence: A Practical Guide*. New York: Henry Holt, 1997.

Seligman, Martin E. P. *Authentic Happiness: Using the New Positive Psychology to Realize Your Potential for Lasting Fulfillment*. New York: Free Press, 2004.

Seligman, Martin E. P. *Learned Optimism: How to Change Your Mind and Your Life*. New York: Vintage, 2006.

Senge, Peter M. *The Fifth Discipline: The Art and Practice of the Learning Organization*. New York: Doubleday Currency, 1994.

Senge, Peter, C. Otto Scharmer, Joseph Jaworski, and Betty Sue Flowers. *Presence: An Exploration of Profound Change in People, Organizations, and Society.* New York: Doubleday Currency, 2005.

Siegel, Daniel J. *The Developing Mind: How Relationships and the Brain Interact to Shape Who We Are.* New York: Guilford Press, 1999.

Sternberg, Esther M. *The Balance Within: The Science Connecting Health and Emotions.* New York: W. H. Freeman and Company, 2001.

Suzuki, D. T. *Essays in Zen Buddhism.* New York: Grove/Atlantic, 1989.

Teilhard de Chardin, Pierre. *The Phenomenon of Man.* San Bernardino, CA: Bongo Press, 1994.

Tichy, Noel M. *The Leadership Engine: How Winning Companies Build Leaders at Every Level.* New York: HarperCollins, 2002.

Tichy, Noel M., and Warren Bennis. *Judgment: How Winning Leaders Make Great Calls.* New York: Portfolio, 2007.

Tzu, Lao. *Tao Te Ching of Lao Tzu.* New York: St. Martin's Press, 1996.

Useem, Michael, and Warren Bennis. *The Leadership Moment: Nine True Stories of Triumph and Disaster and Their Lessons for Us All.* New York: Three Rivers Press, 1998.

Wageman, Ruth, Debra A. Nunes, and James A. Burruss (Center for Public Leadership). *Senior Leadership Teams: What It Takes to Make Them Great.* Boston: Harvard Business School, 2008.

Whyte, David. *The Heart Aroused: Poetry and the Preservation of the Soul in Corporate America.* New York: Doubleday Currency, 1994.

Wilbur, Ken. *No Boundary.* Boston: Shambhala, 1979.

Wilson, Timothy D. *Strangers to Ourselves: Discovering the Adaptive Unconscious.* Cambridge, MA: Harvard University Press, 2002.

Zenger, John H., and Joseph Folkman. *The Extraordinary Leader: Turning Good Managers into Great Leaders.* New York: McGraw-Hill, 2002.

# ACKNOWLEDGMENTS

Writing a book is definitely an odyssey in personal growth. I would encourage you to write "your book," some time in your life, even if it is only for the goal of personal development. It is a very revealing process. It has become apparent to me that writing is less about proclaiming what you know and more about being open to the learning coming your way. I am very grateful for all the learning that has come my way over the years through so many wonderful people. The further I venture into my life journey, the more painfully aware I become of how little I really know and how much others have taught me. I feel very fortunate to be associated with so many growing, gifted human beings.

My warmest, most heartfelt thanks to all the wonderful people at LeaderSource. I am blessed to be with such a brilliant, caring group of people. Special gratitude to Janet Feldman, Bill McCarthy, Renée Garpestad, Faye Way, Katie Cooney, Joe Eastman, Anne Tessien, Sherri Rogalski, Mary Orysen, Sarah Flynn, Pat Costello, Dina Rauker, Lisa Franek, Mike Howe, John Ficken, Stephen Sebastian Cecile Burzynski, Leonard Przybylski, Jody Thone Lande, David Brings, Wayne Dulas, Joan Davis Holly Erickson, Kate Smith, and Erin Olson for all your help, learning, and support in the preparation of this book. Thanks also to Sidney Reisberg, who has passed on since the publication of the first edition, but whose legacy and mentorship live on.

Thanks to my new Korn/Ferry International, Lominger International, and Decision Dynamics colleagues. Since there are hundreds to thank, where do I begin and end? You have welcomed me and LeaderSource with warmth and class to your best-in-the-world firm. Sincere gratitude to Paul Reilly, Gary Burnison, Ana Dutra, Gary Hourihan, Bob Eichinger, Dee Gaeddert, Ken Brousseau, Addy Chulef, Jack McPhail, Francisco Moreno, Marc Swaels, Joachim Kappel, Don Spetner, Tim Dorman, Marti Smye, Mike Distefano, Linda Hyman, Marnie Kittelson, George Hallenbeck, and Ken DeMuese, for all your support, knowledge, and inspiration. I am very fortunate to be associated with all of you, as well as the vast research, resources, and talent that our combined firms represent. Special thanks to Dee and George for the exceptional work on our new Inside-Out/Outside-In Development and Coaching Model. When complete, it will set a new industry standard. This comprehensive approach definitely influenced and moved forward many of the principles of this book. Thanks for your brilliant collaboration!

Thanks to the thousands of clients I have been fortunate enough to serve over the past 30 years. Your gratitude and support have been inspiring, sustaining rewards. I wish I could name all of you, but that would fill up an entire book—thanks for the privilege to know and to serve all of you.

Thanks to Warren Bennis, whom I consider the "godfather of leadership development," a model of the personal and leadership presence I can only aspire to. I want to acknowledge the prodigious, influential work of Jim Collins, author of *Good to Great: Why Some Companies Make the Leap . . . and Others Don't,* and your work in organizational breakthroughs; co-authors of *Primal Leadership: Learning to Lead with Emotional Intelligence* Daniel Goleman, Richard Boyzatis, and Annie McKee, and to Daniel Goleman for bringing emotional intelligence to the world's attention; John Zenger and Joseph Folkman, for your extensive research contributions and your book *Extraordinary Leader: Turning Good Managers into Great Leaders*; Peter Senge, a prominent thought-leader on change and learning and author of *The Fifth Discipline,* as well as co-author of *Presence: An Exploration of Profound Change in Individuals, Organizations and Society;* Robert Hargrove, author of *Masterful Coaching* and your meaningful work in the field of coaching. All of you truly are authentic leaders, whose influence and value creation has been felt around the world.

Thanks to the over 60 CEOs and other executives who shared your thoughts, feelings, and life experiences with me as I prepared the book. Our lively exchanges were helpful, provocative, and insightful. It's a shame CEOs don't take more time to talk about the essence of what they do—thanks for taking the time to do so. Special thanks to Paul Walsh, Ken Melrose, Daniel Vasella, Thomas Ebeling, Bruce Nicholson, Alex Gorsky, Bill George, Corey Seitz, Roger Lacey, David Wessner, Mike Peel, Kevin Wilde, Gus Blanchard, Larry Perlman, Juergen Brokatsky-Geiger, Neil Anthony, Jim Secord, Ron James, David Prosser, John Hetterick, Al Schuman, Bob Kidder, Rob Hawthorne, Chuck Feltz, Robert James, Tom Votel, Mac Lewis, John Sundet, and Tom Gegax for your generous sharing.

Thanks to Ken Shelton, Trent Price, Robert Chapman, and the entire Executive Excellence team for publishing the original edition. Your guidance, persistence, and enthusiasm were crucial to this book when, little more than ten years ago, others found it "too cutting edge." Thanks for partnering with me.

Thanks to everyone at Berrett-Koehler Publishers—Steve Piersanti, Jeevan Simvasubramaniam, Johanna Vondeling, Richard Wilson, Kristen Frantz, Michael Crowley, Katie Sheehan, Jeremy Sullivan, María Jesús Aguiló, David Marshall, and the rest of your exceptional, hard-working team. Thanks to reviewers Barbara Schultz and Jeff Kulick. Sincere gratitude to Debbie Masi, Production Editor, and your team for your extraordinary skill, patience, and commitment to the highest quality. You were my first and only choice as a publishing partner for this new edition. You've broken new ground with your stewardship approach to publishing, and I feel proud, as well as humble, to be among your distinguished family of authors. I appreciate your genuine ardor for my work, but even more so for the authenticity, professionalism and endless humor with which you do yours. You are leading your industry with purpose, vision, and effectiveness.

Incredible thanks to Margie Adler for your editing and research help on this second edition. We had a great time working on the first one, but this new edition would not have happened without you. Your clarity, persistence, consistency, calmness, endurance, and brilliance were amazing. I could not have had a better writing partner on this project. A million thanks.

Thanks to Peggy Lauritsen and her design team for the beautiful cover design on the original and the new edition. For your excellent public relations efforts on the original, thanks to Fred and Sarah Bell Haberman—your excitement and belief in this book always gave me a lift. Thanks to Aaron Berstler and Kohnstamm Communications for your exceptional, professional marketing and public relations assistance on the new book. Thanks to writer-author Jack Forem for your encouragement and friendship. It was your confidence from the moment you told me that I was a "really good writer" that sustained me through a couple of years of drafts. Thanks to James Flaherty for being a "coach's coach" and sharing wisdom with our team.

Special thanks to Bob Silverstein for rejecting my initial manuscript 12 years ago and then sharing with me that I needed to "find my voice." Although I was devastated at first, it was the best feedback I received—it literally transformed my entire approach to writing.

Thanks to Denise, my former spouse, who endured many years of first drafts and rewrites of the original edition. There were many days and weekends, too, when "I couldn't come out to play." The grace with which you granted me leave to create was a precious gift.

My love and gratitude to Soraya, my fiancé, who "prepares multiple places" at home for me to write because I like to move spontaneously from office to bedroom fireplace, or from kitchen table to dining room, as energy moves me. From a family of writers, Soraya knows the value of fostering the creative process. Those quiet, nurturing days you created were a sacrifice for you, but they were so precious for me. Thank you for your help and for your love. Thanks, also, to T. J., my buddy and friend. At age 15, you are an amazing person, truly wise beyond your years, and often my very insightful life coach.

It is impossible to put into words my gratitude for the teacher who influenced my heart, mind, and soul—Maharishi Mahesh Yogi. In the last few days of finishing the manuscript for this edition, this great sage and world teacher left his body. I must acknowledge that there would be no *Leadership from the Inside Out* without Maharishi's inner and outer guidance. His wisdom and practice completely transformed my life. The last time I sat with him he said, "Bring peace and happiness to the world." I hope I have been a worthy student.

My most important thank you goes to you, the reader. I wrote this book for people like you—leaders interested in personal growth and transformation. Thanks for the opportunity to live my purpose with you.

# INDEX

# About the Author

Kevin Cashman is a Senior Partner with Korn/Ferry Leadership and Talent Consulting and founder of LeaderSource, an international development consultancy that became a part of Korn/Ferry in 2006. Over the past twenty-five years and more, Kevin has been involved in coaching and developing thousands of senior executives and senior teams in more than sixty countries. He is recognized as a pioneer in leadership development and executive coaching and was recently names one of the top ten Thought Leaders by *Leadership Excellence* magazine. He is also founder of the Executive to Leader Institute®, acknowledged by *Fast Company* as the "Mayo Clinic" of leadership development for its interdisciplinary approach to leadership development and executive coaching. Between 2006 and 2008, Korn/Ferry International, Lominger International, LeaderSource, and Lore International joined forces to create a premier global leadership and talent consulting practice. Clients include General Mills, Novartis, Bruce Power, Medtronic, Johnson & Johnson, McKinsey and Company, United Way of America, Nokia, Zurich Financial, Rogers Communications, Carlson Companies, and Thrivent Financial.

Kevin is the author of five books on leadership and career development. His book *Leadership from the Inside Out* was named the number-one bestselling business book of 2000 by 1-800-CEO-READ and was also named one of the top twenty bestselling business books of the decade. Kevin has also been featured as a contributing author along with Warren Bennis, Stephen Covey, Marshall Goldsmith, and David Ulrich in the books *A New Paradigm of Leadership* (1997), *Partnering: The New Face of Leadership* (2002), and the upcoming *Leadership Development* (2010). He has written more than a hundred articles and papers on leadership and career management, and has been featured in *The Wall Street Journal, Chief Executive, Human Resource Executive, Fast Company, Strategy & Leadership,* Oprah, CNN, National Public Radio, and other national media. Kevin was formerly the host of *CareerTalk* radio and is currently the leadership columnist for *Forbes.com*.

His second edition of *Leadership from the Inside Out* was published in September 2008 and incorporates the latest research, case studies, and thought leadership gained over the past ten years.

A frequent keynote speaker at conferences and corporate events, Kevin is a Senior Fellow of the Caux Roundtable, a global consortium of CEOs dedicated to enhancing principle-based leadership internationally. He is also a board member for the Center for Ethical Business Cultures fostering ethical leadership in corporations, and is a former board member of Youth Frontiers, bringing character development to more than 100,000 students each year.

Kevin's educational background includes a psychology degree from St. John's University. A believer in dynamic life balance, he has participated in more than fifty triathlons and has practiced and taught meditation for over three decades.

# ABOUT KORN/FERRY LEADERSHIP AND TALENT CONSULTING

Korn/Ferry Leadership and Talent Consulting partners with individuals, teams, and organizations to foster transformative growth and to achieve sustainable organizational performance. We know that talent is at the heart of all successful change efforts. We view leadership and talent development as an ongoing process that must evolve with the company's business objectives, strategies, and culture, as well as the demands and influences of an ever-changing marketplace.

Serving the needs of executives and organizations globally, Korn/Ferry connects talent and strategy to drive sustained performance by partnering with leaders and organizations in three principal offerings: Leadership and Executive Development, Talent and Performance Management Systems, and Strategic and Organizational Alignment. Each of Korn/Ferry's solutions is delivered by an experienced team of leadership consultants, a global network of the top executive coaches, and the intellectual property of research-based, time-tested leadership assessment and developmental tools.

In 2006, Korn/Ferry International, Lominger International, and Lore International began the process of joining forces to create the premier leadership and talent consulting firm in the world with eighty offices spanning forty countries. Clients include General Mills, Novartis, Johnson & Johnson, Bruce Power, McKinsey & Company, Carlson Companies, Nokia, Medtronic, Zurich Financial, Rogers Communications, United Way of America, and Thrivent Financial.

# ABOUT KORN/FERRY
# INTERNATIONAL

It is no longer enough to simply identify and attract the best talent. World-class organizations must now possess the skills to develop, deploy, retain, and reward their best performers—or risk losing them. With a rich history of excellence and innovation in executive recruitment, Korn/Ferry International has expanded its capabilities over the past decade and now provides clients with a proprietary suite of talent management solutions that range from executive recruitment to performance management, recruitment process outsourcing, executive development and coaching, management assessment, and succession planning. These solutions are grounded in decades of research combined with the knowledge and expertise gained firsthand from more than 125,000 engagements.

At Korn/Ferry, the art of a time-tested approach to executive recruitment, a global team of experts, and a deep understanding of the intangibles of leadership are combined with the science of research-based, statistically validated tools and resources. The result is a perspective on human capital that spans the entire employee lifecycle and enables our clients to drive success through the careful and thoughtful management of people.

Korn/Ferry. The Art and Science of Talent.

# Berrett–Koehler
## Publishers

**Berrett-Koehler** is an independent publisher dedicated to an ambitious mission: *Creating a World That Works for All*.

We believe that to truly create a better world, action is needed at all levels—individual, organizational, and societal. At the individual level, our publications help people align their lives with their values and with their aspirations for a better world. At the organizational level, our publications promote progressive leadership and management practices, socially responsible approaches to business, and humane and effective organizations. At the societal level, our publications advance social and economic justice, shared prosperity, sustainability, and new solutions to national and global issues.

A major theme of our publications is "Opening Up New Space." Berrett-Koehler titles challenge conventional thinking, introduce new ideas, and foster positive change. Their common quest is changing the underlying beliefs, mindsets, institutions, and structures that keep generating the same cycles of problems, no matter who our leaders are or what improvement programs we adopt.

We strive to practice what we preach—to operate our publishing company in line with the ideas in our books. At the core of our approach is stewardship, which we define as a deep sense of responsibility to administer the company for the benefit of all of our "stakeholder" groups: authors, customers, employees, investors, service providers, and the communities and environment around us.

We are grateful to the thousands of readers, authors, and other friends of the company who consider themselves to be part of the "BK Community." We hope that you, too, will join us in our mission.

### A BK Business Book

This book is part of our BK Business series. BK Business titles pioneer new and progressive leadership and management practices in all types of public, private, and nonprofit organizations. They promote socially responsible approaches to business, innovative organizational change methods, and more humane and effective organizations.

## Berrett–Koehler Publishers

A community dedicated to creating
a world that works for all

### Visit Our Website: www.bkconnection.com

Read book excerpts, see author videos and Internet movies, read our authors' blogs, join discussion groups, download book apps, find out about the BK Affiliate Network, browse subject-area libraries of books, get special discounts, and more!

### Subscribe to Our Free E-Newsletter, the *BK Communiqué*

Be the first to hear about new publications, special discount offers, exclusive articles, news about bestsellers, and more! Get on the list for our free e-newsletter by going to www.bkconnection.com.

### Get Quantity Discounts

Berrett-Koehler books are available at quantity discounts for orders of ten or more copies. Please call us toll-free at (800) 929-2929 or email us at bkp.orders@aidcvt.com.

### Join the BK Community

BKcommunity.com is a virtual meeting place where people from around the world can engage with kindred spirits to create a world that works for all. BKcommunity.com members may create their own profiles, blog, start and participate in forums and discussion groups, post photos and videos, answer surveys, announce and register for upcoming events, and chat with others online in real time. Please join the conversation!